Character and Virtues:

10 years of
the Jubilee Centre

Aidan P. Thompson

imprint-academic.com

Published in the UK by
Imprint Academic Ltd., PO Box 200, Exeter EX5 5YX, UK

Distributed in the USA by
Ingram Book Company,
One Ingram Blvd., La Vergne, TN 37086, USA

ISBN 9781788360838 paperback
ISBN 9781788360821 hardback

A CIP catalogue record for this book is available from the
British Library and US Library of Congress

Introduction

The Jubilee Centre for Character and Virtues was launched on 16th May 2012 in the House of Lords. It is based at the University of Birmingham, in the School of Education (SoE). Over the subsequent decade, it has established itself as the leading informant on scholarly, policy, and educative matters related to character and virtues, nationally and internationally. Led by Professor James Arthur, to date, it has secured over £25million in research and teaching grants, employed over 70 members of staff, including nine professors and over 30 researchers. The work of the Jubilee Centre has brought together the disciplines of education, philosophy, psychology, sociology and other fields. This book, published during the Jubilee Centre's tenth anniversary year in 2022, documents a history: a history of the chronology of the Jubilee Centre; a history of its people; a history of its research and impact. It is structured in four parts, with Part I capturing the initial planning for the Jubilee Centre's ten-year horizon project, its launch in May 2012, and the Jubilee Journey of major grant phases between 2012 and 2022. Part II then considers the four areas that our work has covered; those of schools, the professions, youth social action, and the specific virtues of gratitude and *phronesis*. Part III looks in more detail at the ways in which we engaged partners and created meaningful impact both in the UK and internationally. The Jubilee Centre has successfully unified the academic field of character and virtues whilst creating tangible impact at education policy-level and on the practice and provision of character education in schools around the world. Part III also discusses Jubilee Centre conferences and events and the impact that they have had on the community of scholars researching character and virtues. Part IV then turns to some reflections on the past ten years, including celebrating some important staff achievements and successes, where the Jubilee Centre has met with challenges and how it set about overcoming and looking towards the future.

As I have taken time to write the history of the Jubilee Centre, it has naturally led me to reflect on my own time in the Jubilee Centre, my own contribution, experiences, and interpretations. My reflections whilst writing have brought me back to memories of events and occasions that I have been part of during the ten years of the Jubilee Centre. I have looked to use some of these as anecdotes to draw out particular points, or add a more personal slant to the organisational history that I present. This book is intended to provide a documentation of how the Jubilee Centre came to be, of the journey on which we have been on since its launch, and act as an archive for the events that have contributed to the elevation of the Jubilee Centre to being the world-leading research centre on character and virtues. Such a claim may seem somewhat grandiose and self-congratulatory when made by a member of the Jubilee Centre's own staff. However, it is important to position the Jubilee Centre accurately before we embark on the Jubilee Journey. The Jubilee Centre is the world-leading research centre on character. That is down to a number of factors, which this book will consider. Firstly, longevity – the Jubilee Centre has been in existence for ten years; there are few that rival our permanency. Secondly, impact – we have sought to create meaningful impact in the societies with which we engage. We, as a staff, are not content to undertake research that simply 'sits on the shelf'. Creating impact is, of course, a necessity of doing academic research, but the Jubilee Centre has embedded its impact strategy at the heart of everything that it does. Thirdly, scope – the Jubilee Centre conducts research and engages with groups on multiple fronts; from schools to universities, from policymakers to practitioners, from professions to charities; the Jubilee Centre conception of character is one that permeates all aspects of culture and society, therefore we aim to undertake research that is relevant to all aspects of society. Fourthly, policy – there are many, many excellent organisations that engage with schools, with young people, with practitioners, professions, and the general public, but without meaningfully managing to influence policy. This is not a criticism, not by any means, but the Jubilee Centre's strategy for engaging multiple stakeholders, especially policymakers, politicians and civil servants, has led to creating impact at a policy level, such as with the Ofsted Inspection Framework (2019), and Department for Education (DfE) (2014-present). Fifth, global engagement – the Jubilee Centre enjoys foreign travel! One of the fundamental principles of the Jubilee Centre's aims is that matters of character are universal. They are relevant to all people, worldwide, and the Jubilee Centre has sought to engage with partners around the world. In fact, much of our global engagement has come from partners reaching out and connecting with us, rather than us reaching out to them. We have more often than not reciprocated and our international work has given us insight into the place of character in different cultures, access to collaborations with researchers looking at related aspects of character, and a breadth of knowledge and understanding that we would not have, had we restricted our engagement. Writing this book serves as a chance for me to acknowledge on behalf of colleagues that we are still learning and that there is still some way to go, for us and for others, given the number of big questions still to be addressed in the field of character education.

These five aspects of the Jubilee Centre's approach since 2012 have contributed to its successes, elevated its position, and created its profile. They do not explain every aspect of the Jubilee Centre's work, its achievements and accomplishments, but they are important strategic elements that have helped shape our approach and our engagement. They are elements on which I intend to reflect more deeply, and draw on examples of the Jubilee Centre's work, as this book progresses. To begin, here, though, I will map out the Jubilee Journey in terms of its major research grants and chronology, which have given structure to the Jubilee Centre's outputs and outcomes, and therefore to the timelines along which colleagues have engaged with partners, practitioners and policymakers.

The Jubilee Centre was not created in a vacuum, and did not emerge from thin air in 2012. There is a history to the work of key members of staff from the Jubilee Centre that predates 2012, work that laid the 'Foundations of Character' on which the Jubilee Centre was constructed. Consideration of this work is vital when charting the history of the Jubilee Centre. The key protagonist here is Professor James Arthur, but the work of Deputy Directors Professors Kristján Kristjánsson and Andrew Peterson and of Dr Tom Harrison has also shaped the Jubilee Journey that we have been on since May 2012. The launch event of the Jubilee Centre on 16th May 2012 at the House of Lords is a major milestone in the Jubilee Centre's history. This is not just because it marked the creation of the Jubilee Centre, but also because of the personnel who attended the launch, the major actors from across a range of sectors, who have since supported the Jubilee Centre. Finally in Part I, I will cast my gaze forward to the 10th anniversary year of celebrations in 2022, and the future of the Jubilee Centre beyond then. We in the Jubilee Centre see 2022 as a major, even *the* major, milestone of our work, which deserves an extended period of celebration and reflection. Writing in advance of such celebrations has allowed me to reflect on the journey so far – writing it down in a way we have not done before. This has been rewarding in a number of ways, but it was also challenging, as I am forecasting and predicting what we will be celebrating and what the future will hold.

In Part II of this book, I turn more closely to the research and impact work of the Jubilee Centre in public life, as we have undertaken it, across four main areas; those being character education in schools, virtuous practice and professional ethics, civic virtue and youth social action, and the meta-virtue of *phronesis*, or practical wisdom. The research that we have conducted in the Jubilee Centre can be categorised under one or more of these themes, and it became a deliberate approach by Management and researchers to focus, extend, and refine research projects across these themes. We have always said that working with schools, with teachers, school leaders, governors and pupils is our 'bread and butter'. It is where the Jubilee Centre began, and where many of our longer-serving members of staff began their careers. The two projects that began in 2011 and 2012 immediately before the first 'Gratitude Britain' phase were large scale, quasi-experimental research trials with young people and teachers in schools. *My Character* and *Knightly Virtues* were projects that worked with many schools across the UK. Indeed, conservative estimates are that the Knightly Virtues teaching resources – that we made freely available after the grant had concluded – have reached 30,000+ students nationally. Both projects sought to combine rigorous research methodologies with large-scale engagement and dissemination, and were important flagstones for the Jubilee Centre to build upon. Both were extremely formative in helping us learn about the ways in which one can undertake research into character in partnership with schools, as well as the challenges and complexities of measurement and evaluation. Since the formal conclusion of both of those projects – both published under the Jubilee Centre's full research portfolio – the Jubilee Centre has engaged with hundreds of school leaders, at thousands of schools, with hundreds of thousands of pupils on character and virtues. We have done so through a concerted and varied programme of research, resources, and engagement. This section of the book looks in more detail at our research with schools, some of our major research findings and how we have utilised them in other projects, disseminated them to create influence and impact, and how we plan to showcase them in our celebrations in 2022.

Part II will also consider the Jubilee Centre's work with the professions, the research that has underpinned the work with doctors, nurses, teachers, lawyers, soldiers, police officers and business professionals, and what the main findings have been for professional ethics, undergraduate training, and practice. The work with the professions has continued into the fourth phase of the Jubilee Centre, the current Celebration Britain phase includes both a wider focus on pre-service training of professionals, and a particular focus on the virtues in policing, and I draw from current findings and insights into the position of ethical training in professional education. The next area that the Jubilee Centre's research has covered is that of civic virtue and social action. The Jubilee Centre was the academic partner to the #iwill campaign, has undertaken research with young people and third sector organisations, and considered what opportunities exist for young people to engage with their communities, whilst developing their own character. Indeed, the Jubilee Centre convened and hosted a consultation on character development and youth social action in 2014 which focussed on the 'double benefit' of youth social action. The double benefit is both the range of capacities that a young person developed in undertaking meaningful social action, while simultaneously building and enhancing the communities with which they engage. Since then, the Jubilee Centre has published two major research reports, including *A Habit of Service*, which found that the younger a person begins their youth social action journey, the more likely they are to continue it beyond school age. As with the work on professional ethics, the Jubilee Centre's interest in civic virtues continues in the Celebration Britain grant phase. Again, this section will draw on current insights from the Jubilee Centre's work, as well as reflections on the most meaningful and enduring research findings from the previous three grant phases. Finally, in Part II, the Jubilee Centre's focus on the specific virtue of gratitude and the meta-virtue of *phronesis* will be explored. These virtues have been given particular attention in our work and our research has created models and measures for the component parts of both virtues.

It is the Jubilee Centre's research work that has formed the substantive element of our portfolio, and that research is framed in a distinctive neo-Aristotelian *Framework* of moral development. Our *Framework* document for schools has proven to be the most impactful publication that we have published – produced and disseminated in consultation and collaboration with scholars, school leaders and practitioners. As with our bank of Statements, the *Framework* was written in collaboration and through discussion, not in an echo chamber on campus. Our neo-Aristotelian approach in which the *Framework* is rooted is neither novel nor unique to only the Jubilee Centre, but we have endeavoured to ensure that we keep it in the centre of our presentation of character, and that we make such a framework relevant to public life in the twenty first century. The *Framework* is not and never has been intended to work as a blueprint for how to 'do' character, in schools or anywhere else. It presents a lens through which schools can view their implicit and explicit character-building activities – many of which are already part of a school day – as character education. *A Framework for Character Education in Schools* was originally conceived of as a document for schools – for school leaders to use as a guide when implementing or refining a character-focus in schools. It was the first published output from the Jubilee Centre in 2013 and has since then gone through three further revisions and iterations. We effectively embarked upon a national consultation with schools and other educational institutions with regards to the *Framework*, to test its relevance, salience and applicability. It has been sent to over 10,000 schools, nationally, and has taken on somewhat of a life of its own in terms of its impact both in and out of education. The Jubilee Centre definition of character education was adopted by both DfE (2014) and Office for Standards in Education, Children's Services and Skills (Ofsted) in England and Wales (2019). Where the Jubilee Centre's research has brought about rigorous findings for what constitutes character, what is understood by it, and how we develop morally, it is the Jubilee Centre's engagement outside of the academy that has brought about much of the impact on education and other fields, as Part III of this book will discuss.

Part III begins with an overview of the impact achieved by the Jubilee Centre since 2012. As with much of the research, the work, though, begins before 2012, and the roots of the Jubilee Centre's impact stem back to previous work by James Arthur and others who would go on to join the Jubilee Centre. It also would not have been possible without the work of the many esteemed academics and practitioners globally who the Jubilee Centre has engaged with via its research, conferences, publications and visits. It has always been a deliberate strategy of the Jubilee Centre's work, as directed by James Arthur, to focus our work on the applicability of character to public life. There seems little point in understanding the philosophy of character, or the psychology of why we do/don't act morally, without seeking to apply that research practically. As Aristotle put it, the purpose of moral inquiry 'is not to know what virtue is, but to become good, since otherwise the inquiry would be of no benefit to us' (Aristotle, *Nichomachean Ethics* [1103b27–29]). Part III looks at the areas in which the Jubilee Centre has created impact and the tools it has used to create engagement and influence. First, I look at the formal partnerships established by the Jubilee Centre with some of the leading research centres, charitable organisations, and schools, globally. We have engaged with each partner differently, and some of the formal partnerships were established for strategic reasons from the outset, whereas others have developed more organically over time. The Jubilee Centre's work with external organisations is not limited to the 24 partnerships listed on its website. We have worked closely with hundreds of schools globally, spoken to tens of thousands of teachers and collaborated with organisations whose reach extends beyond that of the Jubilee Centre. Many of those collaborations developed into formal partnerships, and some of those have been time-bound within a grant phase, or on a particular project. Others have spanned the work of the Jubilee Centre and endured throughout multiple grant phases. In 2012, on launching the Jubilee Centre, we immediately reached out to the pre-eminent research centres on character globally; many of those which based in the United States. We recognised that the work of the likes of Professor Bill Damon (Stanford University), Professor Tom Lickona (Cortland University), Professor Kevin

Ryan and Dr Karen Bohlin (Boston University) and character.org (formerly the Character Education Partnership) by contacting them and inviting them to work with us as we established the Jubilee Centre. We then made connections to centres and organisations elsewhere as the first phase of research began, including centres in Japan, Taiwan, Italy, and at home in the UK.

Part III of the book will reflect on the influence and impact that staff of the Jubilee Centre have created at policy-level with different governments and policymakers globally. As part of the applied nature of the Jubilee Centre's work, we have deliberately strived for both bottom-up and top-down routes to engage stakeholders. Where this section of the book will go on to discuss our work with schools, predominantly in the UK, but also in the US, Italy, Spain, Montenegro, North Macedonia and other countries, it is important to, first, look at the policy impact of our research on character. At home in the United Kingdom, our work with ministers of state, the DfE, Department for Culture, Media and Sport (DCMS), Ofsted, and education policymakers outside of government has been one of the Jubilee Centre's lasting successes. Much of this story is told in *Educating for a Characterful Society* (2020) by James Arthur and co-authors Baroness Morgan of Cotes, Lord James O'Shaughnessy, Sir Anthony Seldon and Dame Julia Cleverdon. Baroness Morgan was Secretary of State for Education (2014-2016) and Secretary of State for Culture, Media and Sport (2019-2020). As Secretary of State (SoS) for

Education, Baroness Morgan formally introduced character education as a focus of the DfE, following meeting with James Arthur and the Jubilee Centre. The formal focus on character still exists in DfE, who have continued to engage the Jubilee Centre through successive Secretaries of State.

The Jubilee Centre has also worked with policymakers and think tanks to ground the academic research in policy language, or enhance it through public opinion polls. Our work with Demos, the leading think tank on character in the UK, has spanned over many years and there is a series of 5 reports that have been published on character, in collaboration with the Jubilee Centre. These range from focussing on the national understanding of character, through character and service learning and social action, to character in the digital world of social media. Such publications have been launched at political party conferences, with guest speakers including MPs and leading policymakers. The intention behind collaborating with Demos and other think tanks has always been to maximise the reach of the Jubilee Centre's work, to extend the importance of character across areas that the Jubilee Centre may not be engaging in directly, or increasing existing areas of focus. The Jubilee Centre is politically neutral in its approach, and we have sought to engage both the political left and the political right in matters of character. Character is a matter of universal concern, regardless of demographics or political affiliation; hence, the Jubilee Centre has sought to work with partners across sectors, faiths, and politics. These have included religious organisations (including the Church of England, Catholic Education Service, as well as educational organisations with ties to Jewish communities, Muslim schools, and other faiths); the Conservative, Labour and Liberal Democrat parties; as well as other academic centres, charities, and non-profit organisations, nationally. Internationally, the Jubilee Centre has advised governments in Montenegro, North Macedonia, Japan, Singapore, the Vatican, Argentina, Colombia, to name a few. One of our leading partnerships has been with UNICEF, particularly working in Montenegro and North Macedonia, but also extending across the Balkans, and beyond. The work with schools in Montenegro, and with UNICEF, is a good example of how the research of the Jubilee Centre, conducted in the Great Britain, has been applied with an international audience.

Similarly, the Jubilee Centre has engaged with schools and practitioners in over 50 countries. Many of those have been via face-to-face conference presentations, such as those given by colleagues in Mexico, Malaysia, United States and Germany, but also via the online Continuing Professional Development (CPD) programme *Leading Character Education in Schools* that launched in April 2020. The CPD programme brings together the research findings of the Jubilee Centre's work with schools and school leaders in the UK since 2012, and provides a resource for teachers looking to embark or embed a character focus in their schools. The programme is the Jubilee Centre's offer to teachers and school leaders in response to the question that we have been asked repeatedly 'how do I do it?'. Teachers require no convincing that they are character educators of the pupils in their care. However, teachers, in the UK especially, are required to do so much additional administration and other work that they see providing for character education as another thing to add to their already full plate. To continue the metaphor, the Jubilee Centre has always strived to equip teachers with treating character not as an additional item to add onto the plate, but to conceive of it as the plate itself – and the CPD programme provides insights, tools, and advice for how teachers can enhance their provision, regardless of where they are on their character journeys. It is the summative output of three grant phases, all of which has been building towards providing teachers with such an offer. Where the other teaching resources, inclusion and involvement in active research, and even our own MA Character Education programme, have provided opportunities for teachers to engage with character, the CPD programme is more comprehensive than any other resource that the Jubilee Centre has produced. It is something that, as we celebrate our tenth anniversary, that we hope will endure as a resource for developing leaders of character.

Our work with schools, as I introduced above, has been the bedrock of the Jubilee Centre's research, and of its successes, in terms of impact and engagement. Alongside our work with schools, our annual conference, held at Oriel College, Oxford, has become the pre-eminent international conference on character. We began with our first conference in December 2012 (held in Birmingham) as the first major event that the Jubilee Centre had hosted. This was six months after Gratitude Britain had started, and three months after we had recruited our team of researchers and professional services personnel. Each year, the conference has embraced a different theme within the broad field of character and virtues and assembled a line-up of keynote and seminar presentations from the leading thinkers and practitioners from around the world. Most of our conferences have led to the publication of proceedings as edited volumes with top publishers or special issues of leading journals. It is an event that we in the Jubilee Centre look forward to each year, and are proud of what it has become. Luminaries in the world of character request to attend every year, even if they do not present papers, as it has become a place where the latest research findings can be shared, constructive but critical feedback is sought, and professional friendships are established.

In addition to the Jubilee Centre annual conference, we have convened and hosted numerous other conferences since 2012. The Jubilee Centre has held a bi-annual conference (every two years) on a different theme related to character, beginning in 2014 with a Seminar on Gratitude. Further conferences have engaged those in the professions (2016), the arts (2018), and whilst the Covid-19 pandemic halted events in 2020, there are plans to resume such focussed conferences in the coming months. These bi-annual conferences have brought delegates together from an array of disciplines and backgrounds and focussed discussions through the lens of the Jubilee Centre's work. They have led to the publication of conference proceedings as edited collections, as well as generating engagement and extending the Jubilee Centre's network. The partnership with US Military Academy West Point began as a result of delegates attending the 'Character and Virtues in the Professions' conference in June 2016, and has extended to delegations from USMA West Point visiting the Jubilee Centre, visits to New York to speak to cadets, and James Arthur being made a Senior Fellow of USMA.

As well as running traditional academic conferences, the Jubilee Centre has hosted multiple consultations on particular topics related to character that have served to underpin the content of the series of Statements published. These include Statements on youth social action, civic virtue, professional ethics and sport. The consultations have brought together leading academics, policymakers and practitioners to debate and discuss the key themes related to character. Such consultations and their subsequent statements have engaged audiences outside of the academy, and brought the language of character to bear on areas of interest to the Jubilee Centre. In addition to these consultations, the Jubilee Centre has also hosted multiple practitioner conferences, community days, and other activities to engage teachers, school leaders and students on matters of character. In particular, in the early years of the Jubilee Centre, we set about a full development programme of activities to engage young people on gratitude and on service. Other significant events have included a one-day teacher conference on the revised Ofsted Education Inspection Framework (EIF) (2019), two 'Character Matters' events that brought leading politicians and persons from public life to the University of Birmingham to speak to staff and students, and the Thank You Film and Letter Awards and the Jubilee Awards for Service. Part III of this book brings together the strategies employed behind such conferences and events in order to maximise the engagement and impact of the Jubilee Centre.

Part IV of the book draws together the reflections on what has come in the three previous parts, before summarising the main successes of the Jubilee Centre since 2012. It will also reflect on some individual achievements of members of the Jubilee Centre team. Since 2012, the Jubilee Centre has employed over 70 people, and engaged well over 200 consultants. During that period, as the work of the Jubilee Centre has achieved success, so have the individuals who have made it happen. Staff have received honours from the Queen, studied for postgraduate degrees and been awarded Fellowships. As we celebrate the tenth anniversary of the Jubilee Centre, it is important to acknowledge the achievements and efforts of the staff members who have made it all happen. The Jubilee Centre adopted a strategy of recruiting the very best early career research and professional service staff that it could find, and many of those individuals have gone on to become the leading lights in character teaching and research in the UK and abroad. The management of the Jubilee Centre has benefitted from a settled team that have worked together over a significant period, and each of whom has contributed to the consistency, longevity and durability of the Jubilee Centre. Of course, it has not all been plain sailing, and the penultimate section of Part IV will reflect on the major challenges that the Jubilee Centre has faced since its creation, but also on the major challenges ahead in continuing its work. Finally, I conclude with a look forward to 2023 and beyond, acknowledging the unfinished nature of working in the field of character and virtues, and projecting what the future of the Jubilee Centre may hold.

Whilst this book is sole-authored, I could not write this book alone, and I have drawn on the many individual and organisational connections and partnerships that the Jubilee Centre has established to engage and involve as many perspectives and reflections as has been possible during 2022. The book is written from one perspective; mine, but it includes anecdotes, events and musings that involve many colleagues and former colleagues in the Jubilee Centre, as well as key partners and friends. We are not immune to criticism and in acknowledging the challenges that we have faced at each stage of the Jubilee Journey, I have sought to reflect on some of the criticisms and challenges that we have faced. We are, though, our own biggest critic and I have sought to capture some of the internal debates and dilemmas that we have faced that would otherwise go unreported. This is in an effort to give an honest and open account of what the Jubilee Journey has really been like to have been part of. I was honoured when I was asked to write this book on behalf of James and the whole Jubilee Centre, so I hope that what follows does justice to the Journey we have been on since 2012.

I

History
and Chronology

2012 – Launch of the Jubilee Centre
for Character and Virtues

Part I of this book begins on 16th May 2012, in the Attlee Room of the House of Lords, at the launch of a new research centre to be based in the School of Education at the University of Birmingham; the Jubilee Centre for Character and Values. In attendance were a number of delegates who had an interest in character and character education, as well as dignitaries representing the House of Lords, University of Birmingham, and the Director of the new research centre. The launch came during the diamond jubilee year of Queen Elizabeth II, and marked the creation of the first research centre dedicated to researching character in the UK. Today, it remains the only research centre dedicated to character in the UK. Lord Watson of Richmond hosted the launch event. He had served as the Chair of the Advisory Board to a previous study of character led by James Arthur called Learning for Life (2005-2010). Speakers at the event included Professor Sir David Eastwood, Vice-Chancellor of the University of Birmingham (2009-2021), and Dr Jack Templeton, President of the John Templeton Foundation, the philanthropic organisation that were funding the creation of the Jubilee Centre. Also in attendance were delegates from schools, businesses, policy and the third sector – largely contacts made through Learning for Life, and who we had begun to engage through subsequent projects with schools. We came together to launch the Jubilee Centre, and share their interest in character and virtues. Many of those in attendance would go on to form partnerships and collaborate with us on research and practical programmes. The Jubilee Centre would go on to change its name to the Jubilee Centre for Character and Virtues after its initial work, particularly with schools, uncovered greater confidence and commitment to the language of virtue that we had first anticipated.

The launch event itself took place on a sunny Wednesday in Westminster, London. Holding the launch at the House of Lords reflected the prestige of the occasion and the seriousness and the importance with which the funder, University, and all other stakeholders were placing on this new endeavour. The Learning for Life Advisory Board, made up of business leaders, politicians, educationalists and third sector workers, had provided advice and guidance to the project, as well as access to venues and events. The project had held previous report launches in Parliament, and remained in contact with the Advisory Board after the end of that project, particularly Lord Watson, and so we asked if he would host on the day. Of course, when seeking to engage stakeholders in one's work, particularly potential new partners, inviting them to a prestigious venue, to the launch of a research centre dedicated to a topic they have some knowledge of and interest in helps get people's attention. Lord Watson departed soon after the event had concluded – rushing to a BBC radio studio to be interviewed on the 'PM' programme about the launch of a new research centre focussed on character. The Jubilee Centre was attracting attention from the off!

The planning of the formal launch event took place over just a few weeks. Indeed, the opportunity to establish a full research centre dedicated to character came about very quickly in late 2011 and early 2012. Whilst there had been some conversations as early as 2010 – one particular conversation took place between James Arthur and Jack Templeton the morning after a major dinner at St Ann's College in Oxford. James had recently published *Of Good Character* (2010) as the summative report for the Learning for Life project and Jack Templeton was keen to build on the successes of that work by creating a longer-term project in Britain dedicated to character. The guest list for the launch was drawn largely from connections that had been established through the other work on character – Learning for Life, *My Character* and *Knightly Virtues*. *My Character* and *Knightly Virtues* were both live research projects at the time of the launch, and both had built significant networks of practitioners, academics and policymakers. Many of the delegates in attendance had cleared their diaries in order to attend, recognising the potential significance of the occasion, and what the Jubilee Centre was being created to do in Britain.

The investment in research into character and virtues provided by the John Templeton Foundation (JTF) did not begin with the grant that established the Jubilee Centre. The JTF has a long history of investing in innovative and rigorous research and entrepreneurial projects that collect big data and answer big questions. The size of the research grants being awarded to academics globally to look at different aspects of character and virtues was growing, marking the significant interest of both funders and of academics in character and virtues. In securing grants that totalled an initial £6.3m, and with a commitment from JTF to fund the Jubilee Centre for a ten-year period (total funding of over £21m), the launch event of the Jubilee Centre needed to be one which reflected the scale, importance, and significance of what would come. I will say more in Part III and Part IV about how the Jubilee Centre has sought to use the funding that it has secured to maximise the outputs, engagement and impact.

Reflecting on the last ten years, and looking back to that launch event, it would not have been possible to predict the extent and scale of the reach and impact that the Jubilee Centre has since achieved. However, there were indications of the level of expectation that were being placed on the Jubilee Centre, and which James Arthur was placing on himself and his (still to be appointed) team, in the speeches given by Sir David Eastwood, Jack Templeton and Lord Watson. Each of the three main speakers at the launch spoke about the importance of prioritising character in education, and the significance of dedicating a research centre to looking at matters of character would help bring that priority to the fore.

The first phase of the Jubilee Centre's work was titled 'Gratitude Britain', following the four themes identified by Dr Jack Templeton in Queen Elizabeth's jubilee speech from 2012 – the others following as 'service', 'transformation', and 'celebration'. In highlighting the virtue of gratitude, Dr Templeton called on the Jubilee Centre to honour his father, Sir John Templeton, whom he said saw gratitude 'as the glue that keeps people and civilisation and people together.' In aiming to set the Jubilee Centre up to become a major international hub of inter-disciplinary research into not only gratitude but overall character and virtues, everyone involved needed to recognise the significance of the launch and of what was being expected of the research that would follow from Jubilee Centre staff. Once the team had been fully recruited and inducted, the Jubilee Centre would hold its full launch at its inaugural conference in December 2012.

Of course, such a launch event, and such an opportunity to undertake serious and meaningful research on some of philosophy's biggest questions on what it is to live a good life, do not materialise out of the ether. They come from years of work establishing foundations of research findings that have formed the basis on which the Jubilee Centre was constructed. This work will be explored in greater depth in the next section of Part I, but begins with the 5-year Learning for Life project, led by James Arthur, and funded by the John Templeton Foundation (2005-2010). Subsequent research grants from JTF for *My Character* and *Knightly Virtues* provided a platform, both academically and operationally, to establish a larger research centre. The experience of leading an extensive and long-term project, Learning for Life, had equipped James Arthur with many of the necessary skills and expertise to run a research project on the scale that was being set up for the Jubilee Centre. That project had sought to create influence and impact on a national scale, engaging practitioners and policymakers, and had achieved many successes. Then, in being able to immediately incorporate live research projects, those of *My Character* and *Knightly Virtues*, into the Jubilee Centre on its launch created a sense of real momentum and visible action from the outset. These projects were researching the direct link between theory and practice in character education and beginning to explore the idea of 'what works' in the classroom, which helped our new team of researchers see what type of work would be expected of them, as the creation of the Jubilee Centre showed the schools involved in those two projects that they were part of something much larger.

At the time of the launch on 16th May 2012, and even when the research grant formally began on 1 June 2012, the only employee of the Jubilee Centre was Professor James Arthur, Director. As James states in his case study of the Jubilee Centre in his book *Policy Entrepreneurship in Education* (2018), it would take a number of months to fully staff the Jubilee Centre, but a number of those who have featured prominently in the work of the Jubilee Centre since were also there on that day. James recruited Professor David Carr, already working on the *Knightly Virtues* project, and Tom Harrison, who moved from the core Learning for Life team and a consultant on *Knightly Virtues* and on *My Character*, and myself. I officially became the Jubilee

Centre's first Centre Manager on 1st September 2012. The first external appointment was that of Professor Kristján Kristjánsson as Deputy Director (Research), who would take the Chair in Character Education and Virtue Ethics. This in itself was a significant moment as it was only the second professorship dedicated to character in the world – the other being held by Professor Marvin Berkowitz at the University of Missouri-St. Louis. Each of these individuals brought their own experience and interest in character and virtues to the newly formed Jubilee Centre.

The Summer of 2012 was then spent recruiting a team of Research Fellows and Professional Services staff to join the Jubilee Centre from Autumn 2012 to undertake its portfolio of research and development activities. The initial themes of the Jubilee Centre's work endure through to today's research, with a concentration of activities around character education in schools, virtues in the professions, youth social action and service, and *phronesis* (practical wisdom). Initial projects sought to break new ground and collect big datasets, with *Character Education in UK Schools* and *An Attitude for Gratitude* both engaging over 10,000 participants during the initial grant phase (June 2012 – February 2015).

It would be easy to retell the story of the Jubilee Centre in a chronological way, beginning with its launch at the House of Lords on 16th May 2012, and taking things forward through successive grant phase, Gratitude Britain, Service Britain and Transformative Britain, up to the current Celebration Britain phase of work, as we prepare for our 10-year anniversary in 2022. However, such an approach would be limited as it would fracture the description of the different areas of focus that the Jubilee Centre has excelled in; particularly those of character education, work with the professions, overall research objectives and impact on policy. So, I will begin with a short, plotted history of key events, before later chapters take a thematic approach to reflecting on the past ten years. This is intended to provide a reflection on the scope and breadth of the work of the Jubilee Centre, rather than limiting it to a series of milestones or key events, described in order.

Indeed, as introduced above, the Jubilee Centre did not simply come to be in 2012. It was the culmination of many years of endeavour, research and scholarship that led to the creation of the Jubilee Centre, both by those leading the project – James Arthur, Kristján Kristjánsson, Tom Harrison, David Carr – and those creating the opportunity to launch a centre dedicated to character in the UK in 2012.

I have mentioned the JTF research projects that James Arthur led on prior to 2012. Understanding them in a little more detail and context can help paint the picture as to why creating a large, inter-disciplinary research centre dedicated to character made sense. Further, the work of David Carr and Kristján Kristjánsson on virtues, moral education and a neo-Aristotelian approach to character – predating the Jubilee Centre by a decade or two – gave the Jubilee Centre incredibly strong foundations on which to begin its research and to base its own understanding of character. This neo-Aristotelian definition of character, and philosophy of virtues has endured throughout the 10 years that the Jubilee Centre has been in existence, with the Jubilee Centre's research adding weight to existing understandings, and breaking new ground in the field. The Jubilee Centre sought very early on to extend formal partnership invitations to some of the leading research centres and individual scholars in the field, from the US, Far East, and Europe, to work collaboratively. During the past ten years, we have welcomed visits from and visited all of the leading lights in character and virtues studies, from Annas to Berkowitz, from Bohlin to Curren, from Snow to Miller, from Fowers to Lickona, and many more. In addition to the individuals and their research interested in character and virtues, the JTF has a long history of dedicating significant funding to character research, around the world. This research has combined theoretical understandings with empirical data, crossing disciplines and answering some of the big questions about what it is to live well and flourish. It is from these strong foundations that the Jubilee Centre based its research portfolio, as it sought to advance the understandings of not just its own staff, but those working in the field globally. The next section will explore some of the foundations that the Jubilee Centre built upon.

Building on the Foundations of Character (pre-2012)

There is clearly a place and purpose in beginning with a historical chronology that maps out some major milestones which can be used to contextualise both the major achievements of the Jubilee Centre and of the growth in interest in character in all aspects of public life. This chapter is structured to begin with such a plotted history, from the launch of the Jubilee Centre in May 2012, through to plans for the 2022 10th anniversary. This section will cast its gaze backwards to pre-2012 events and research that helped lay the foundations on which the Jubilee Centre was constructed. The main focus is, of course, on the work of the Jubilee Centre, its achievements, research, impact and influence. However, there are important external developments and milestones that are worthy of mention, as they provide context and rationale for why the Jubilee Centre prioritised particular activities, pursued particular lines of enquiry, and developed particular partnerships at different times. Examples of such milestones include the national prioritisation of character by the DfE in England and Wales in 2014 under Baroness Nicky Morgan, and the inclusion of character under 'personal development' in the Ofsted EIF in 2019. The Jubilee Centre team made significant contributions to both of these milestones, through conversation with ministers and civil servants, and citation of research findings, which has, in turn, led to more schools prioritising character education as a good in and of itself. At the time, there was no coherent language of character being used in any meaningful way in DfE, nor with Ofsted. It is somewhat remarkable, looking back, that it has been given so much attention by DfE, Secretaries of State, and Ofsted. Internationally, research grant opportunities provided by organisations such as the JTF and the Kern Family Foundation (KFF) that specifically prioritise character have grown the global network of character researchers and educators. JTF has a long history of funding character research, and is one of the most important foundations on which the Jubilee Centre's creation is built, and but the continued and growing interest in matters of character, enabled and facilitated by funding provided by JTF and others, has strengthened the academic understanding of character, what it is, how it can be developed, and what the differences in how it is understood globally.

Such milestones, as well as countless others, have helped cement character as a serious and important focus of academic research, and of educational purpose. The Jubilee Centre has always prioritised both in its aims and in outcomes. Such aims were stated upon the launch of the Jubilee Centre in 2012, and remain today. In 2012, in Great Britain, society was recovering from a summer (2011) of riots, of (then) unprecedented social change, and of calls for education to be reimagined. Many of these calls remain today, ten years on, but then there was very little by way of the use of the language of character in any conversation on education, on social mobility, or on preparing young people to contribute meaningfully to society. James Arthur had joined an inquiry assembled by the London-based think tank Demos on character in 2010-2011, which looked at the role of character in relation to wellbeing, social mobility and education. *The Character Inquiry* (2011) stated that 'character should be at the heart of our responses to social problems...'. Such a call pre-dated the summer riots of 2011, but it has endured the test of time – possibly as relevant today as ten years ago. That is not to say that nothing has changed about the place of character in conversations about society – indeed, just the opposite. Our work has created in stakeholders a familiarity with the language of character and virtue so that they can speak to one another with a shared understanding of what character is, what it means in society, particularly to young people, and the importance of making space and enabling provision for meaningful character development in education. This is one of our most significant pieces of impact – that we can speak about character and virtues with young people, teachers, parents and policymakers from a generally shared position of what is meant by 'character' and 'character education', and that there is a shared recognition that developing good character is a good this in education. Such a priority for character simply was not there on any sort of national level in 2012.

To begin our work, though, the Jubilee Centre team needed to be familiar with the language of character as it set out on its mission to undertake meaningful and rigorous research in 2012. The name of the centre, the Jubilee Centre for Character and Values, linked in part to the year of the Queen's Diamond Jubilee and in part to prioritising central focus character. In 2012, in British education landscape was one that was ready to embrace more of a focus on educating the whole child, moving away from an over-prioritisation of academic attainment. That said, there was some perceived resistance and hesitance to embracing a neo-Aristotelian approach to virtue, wholesale. We settled on the name 'character and values' as it embraced both the notion of character as the Jubilee Centre's chief research subject, and the language of values which was both one familiar to schools, and one which educationalists were already comfortable with. As Lord James O'Shaughnessy maps out in his chapter of the 2020 book *Educating for a Characterful Society*, government and education policymakers in the lead up to 2012 were beginning to move beyond the prioritisation of academic attainment and focus on fixing perceived poor behaviour that had come before. James Arthur's research background positioned him in 2012 as the UK's leading academic on character. His publications history reflects this, with his 2003 book *Education with Character* being written, at least in part, to address the then Labour government's policy of 'promoting education with character'. At the time, any focus on character was very much wrapped up in improving attainment and ensuring that students were employable outside of the classroom. However, in drawing attention to the character-focus of the government's policy, in keeping character central in the discourse on what schooling is for, what constitutes a good life and that developing positive character traits should be seen as a positive educational outcome in its own right.

Since the 2003 book, Arthur has gone on to write dozens of books, papers and other publications on character, most recently authoring *The Formation of Character in Education: From Aristotle to the 21st Century* (2019), *Educating for a Characterful Society: Responsibility and the Public Good* (2020) and *A Christian Education in the Virtues: Character Formation and Human Flourishing* (2021). All of these titles, and the work that James has pioneered, have ensured that character has remained on the policy agenda in the UK, had major impact and influence internationally, and most have been direct outputs of the JTF funding that created and sustained the Jubilee Centre. The range of publications published by the Jubilee Centre's team engages a range of stakeholders; from books for young children that focus on particular virtues, through textbooks for university students, practical books for teachers, professionals, and parents. They are in addition to the academic publications that have considered huge datasets, new philosophical thinking, and frameworks for contemplating what character is and what a focus on developing good character is for. As the founding Director, James's work that laid strong foundations for all of which was to follow. James is a qualified teacher, and taught in a Catholic boys' school in Birmingham before going to the University of Oxford to study for an MSc and D.Phil. During and after those studies, James engaged multiple scholars, practitioners and policymakers on themes linked to character, values, citizenship and communitarianism. Included in those names were people such as Karen Bohlin, Kevin Ryan,

and other influential people in the field of character –
particularly in the 1980s and 1990s. In his early
publications, Arthur emphasised character from a
policy dimension – as used by the Labour opposition
(pre-1997) and the Labour government in their early
years in office. In addition to the policy dimension, the
Learning for Life project (2005-2010) emphasised the
practical dimension to enabling and facilitating
character education with young people and in schools.
At the time, *Learning for Life* was the UK's largest
study of the virtues and values of young people aged
3-25 years. Combining those audiences of practitioners
and young people and policymakers, whilst ensuring
academic rigour and scholarly originality, existed in
work before the Jubilee Centre was launched, but has
been a foundational principle of all of the research that
would come from 2012 onwards.

In addition to James, Kristján Kristjánsson's
work was well established in its focus on the
philosophy of virtue and neo-Aristotelian conceptions
of emotion, virtue, and the self. Kristjánsson joined the
Jubilee Centre in 2012 as one of the leading neo-
Aristotelian scholars, globally. Together, the academic
foundations that Arthur and Kristjánsson had laid as
individual scholars provided a resolute and rigid base
from which the Jubilee Centre was born.
Kristjánsson's work on *Aristotle, Emotions, and
Education* (2007) and *The Self and Its Emotions* (2010)
complimented the focus on character education in
schools and education policy that James had
established in the UK. Kristján's work, supplemented

by that of others such as Tom Harrison and Andrew Peterson, helped the newly appointed team of researchers hit the ground not just running, but almost sprinting in terms of working from an explicit framework for character and virtues. Such a framework was articulated in the Jubilee Centre's first publication in 2013 with the first iteration of *A Framework for Character Education in Schools*, a publication that I will return to later.

The Jubilee Centre's main focus of research, influence and impact has been education and schools. This work with schools began before 2012 with *My Character* and *Knightly Virtues*, and also with *Learning for Life*, a research grant that James Arthur led 2005-2010, and moved to Birmingham in 2009 for its final 12 months. *Learning for Life* was a project that looked at the character and values of 3-25-year olds across different educational and professional settings. Centred on a notion of character and values, and seeking to build on the existing body of literature around values education, the project broke new ground in collecting data across 5 distinct age groups of participants. From early years to university graduates, it was the UK's largest study of character and values. In addition to collecting a large dataset, though, it sought to elucidate more clearly what those involved in the debate meant by the language of character that they used. From young people to young adults, from teachers to parents, the study found that participants were comfortable using the language of character with some ease, but that terms were often used interchangeably with others, or with different meanings. The language of character education is not fixed, and the study found that many terms, including the word 'character' were used in different senses, by different contributors, and for different purposes. However, all were used under what can be described as a general umbrella of positive traits and living well. *Learning for Life* presented research that offers some suggestions about possible ways forward in developing concrete proposals for moral education, in particular in identifying an appropriate language that can be used by practitioners in situations 'on the ground'.

Learning for Life was both an evolutionary and revolutionary project, in terms of character education research in Great Britain. Studies on the scale achieved by the project had not been done in Britain before, with over 25,000 young people involved across the 5 projects. Its findings were disseminated to practitioners, and used to inform government and policymakers across education. It was not only its findings that were revolutionary – showing how important it is to base understandings of character in a clear and articulated framework and language in order to share understanding and consensus on what character is and how to educate for it. Its mixed methods approach to data collection provided a strong and rigorous benchmark that all future Jubilee Centre research has sought to match or surpass. Combining large scale empirical surveys with smaller scale, in-depth qualitative interviews, focus groups and observations allowed empirical findings to be supported by rich quotes and case studies. Such mixed methods research has since become the norm and standard across the social sciences since *Learning for Life* began in 2005, and particularly in studies of character education. Many of the Jubilee Centre's subsequent projects drew from the foundations created by the *Learning for Life*. The work with schools, for example, particularly in terms of creating a database of schools that were explicitly prioritising a focus on character, helped projects such as *My Character* and *Knightly Virtues* find warm participants, as well as providing a baseline of understanding of the benefits to prioritising a character focus in schools that researchers could turn to. The early flagship research project in the Gratitude Britain phase of Jubilee Centre work used experiences of surveying pupils and teachers in schools, running focus groups with younger pupils and interviewing older students to help inform the overall project approach. The *Character Education in UK Schools* project surveyed 10,000 participants in a little over 2 years, and found some interesting supporting and contrasting findings to the *Learning for Life* work.

These foundations were not just limited to the research, methods, or participants. Much of the dissemination and influence that was created by James Arthur and his *Learning for Life* team was moved forward into the Jubilee Centre's work. The Advisory Board that had been established continued to provide advice, guidance, and, where appropriate, access to stakeholders across education. The success of the *Learning for Life* project provided the Jubilee Centre team with some initial access to policymakers, civil servants and politicians who were already familiar with and open to the idea that character should be treated as a good in and of itself in schools. It was vital to see good character not as a fix for poor behaviour in the classroom, or as a way of ensuring high attainment in exams, but something that should be valued in and of itself. The main change at policy level during that period, though, was the change of government in 2010, from a Labour one to a Conservative/Liberal Democrat coalition government. The Jubilee Centre followed *Learning for Life* in being non-partisan, or seeing character as a-political, or non-political, in policy terms, and seeking to engage those from the political left and right in its work. The Advisory Board that was inherited from *Learning for Life* included politicians from each of the three main political parties. Since 2012, whilst there has remained a Conservative government, the Jubilee Centre has continued to engage both sides, and found that both sides see character in largely similar terms. It is fair to say that the Jubilee Centre's most tangible examples of positive impact, such as those with DfE and Ofsted, were secured in part due to the groundwork done pre-2012.

In particular, *Knightly Virtues* was a project that caught the attention of policymakers, in part for its use of stories to engage more explicit conversation on character with Key Stage 2 pupils (9-11-year olds), but also because of the clear definitions of what character is and which virtue terms were being prioritised in the project. The *Knightly Virtues* definition of character, for example, was adopted at a DfE meeting of civil servants, the Secretary of State, James Arthur and other notable education stakeholders, due to its clarity, simplicity, and an absence of competing alternatives. The Jubilee Centre, in recognising an existing incoherence in the language of character and virtue in the classroom and amongst scholars, set out to clarify terms, provide definitions, and aid understanding, all of which, at that point, was beginning to impact not just the classroom, but education policy overall.

Providing a clear, concise and articulate language of character was only the first step, though, if the Jubilee Centre was to meet its lofty initial aims to be the leading scholarly research centre in the field, and also to impact the practice of developing character in schools, universities, and professional places of work. As well as a clear and coherent language, the research would need to be rigorous and robust, collecting as it does large datasets of mixed methods data. The findings would need to be presented in scholarly and also in lay terms, proving their academic worth without losing practitioners along the way by being overly philosophical, impractical, or unrepresentative. And the dissemination of the findings would need to show how and why character should be regarded as a positive educational outcome in and of its own right, rather than simply as a means through which behaviour can be improved, or attainment targets can be reached.

The Jubilee Journey

The first research phase of the Jubilee Centre – Gratitude Britain – began on 1st June 2012. The 'Jubilee Journey' began before then, though, as the previous sections have laid out. The Jubilee Centre was not created out of the ether, but was a culmination of years of research, led by James Arthur, but contributed to by others. That said, in bringing together a team of leading scholars and early career researchers and administrators in one place for the first time, to embark on a dedicated programme of work was not only a significant moment for those involved, but one that is now being recognised and remembered ten years later.

Once a core leadership team had been established – of James Arthur, Kristján Kristjánsson, David Carr, Tom Harrison and myself – in the Summer of 2012, the next task was to recruit and select a team of researchers and administrators to operationalise the first programme of work. This began with a large recruitment campaign, with adverts placed in national newspapers such as the *Times Higher Education*, *Guardian*, as well as on academic job platforms. It was followed by a week of back-to-back interviews for research posts, before the team first came together in September 2012. A small number of the original team would join throughout the autumn term in 2012, but it was that first meeting of new starters in the School of Education at the University of Birmingham where we could begin properly with the Gratitude Britain phase of work. This first 'induction' meeting is one that we have ended up repeating at the beginning of every subsequent phase of work – Service Britain, Transformative Britain, Celebration Britain – with new and continuing staff each time, but this first induction in 2012 brought everyone together in new roles, in a new centre, and for many, in a new city. It was also a good test as just a few days later, we were visited by Drs Jack and Pina Templeton from the JTF, who visited Birmingham to see how the grant had begun. We met on a Sunday in early September in one of the now refurbished conference rooms in Hornton Grange, just up the road from the main campus. It was Jack and Pina's first (and only) visit to Birmingham. It was an important meeting – we were under no illusions of the need to impress. It was also the first time that many of us had been into 'work' at the University on a Sunday! It was a good meeting, full of robust discussion, as well as presenting our initial thoughts as a research centre on character and virtues. I recall Jack speaking at length about the virtue of gratitude during the meeting, as the focus of the grant phase, and everyone from the Jubilee Centre recognised then, if they had not already, the significance of the work that they would be undertaking.

There can sometimes be a conception that the Jubilee Centre began with a clean slate, with regards to how it theorised and defined 'character' and other key terms and conceptions – that we began with nothing and created from 2012 onwards. This is not the case, as the previous section of this chapter has sought to pre-empt and address. As outlined above, James Arthur had been writing on character for some ten years before the launch of the Jubilee Centre. Kristján Kristjánsson, too, has a fifteen-year publication history that pre-dates the Jubilee Centre. David Carr had an already well-established and distinguished academic career when he joined the University of Birmingham shortly before the Jubilee Centre launched. Andrew Peterson has written on civic virtue and civic education for much of the past decade. Equally, Tom Harrison, although at the beginning of his academic career at that time, had experience of developing character in youth and voluntary organisations. The focus on a neo-Aristotelian conception of character was always intended to bring Aristotle into the twenty-first century. Other criticisms of the Jubilee Centre over the past ten years have suggested that the Jubilee Centre definition of character and virtues is simply derived from Aristotle's *Nicomachean Ethics*. Again, this is not true, and whilst we are a neo-Aristotelian centre, the work of the Jubilee Centre has always sought to critique, evaluate and synthesise the existing literature. Our conception of character takes the most enduring and relevant parts of Aristotle, and of Arthur, Kristjánsson, Carr, then also of the conservative theories of character education (see

Bennett, Lickona or Ryan), adaptations of more recent liberal conceptions of character education (see Berkowitz), and build on other views from other academic disciplines and public discourse. We have always sought to engage policymakers on the political right and left, as character is a term that both the political left and right have engaged with. The dissemination and impact strategies that we have adopted have created impact at policy level in a number of countries, and engaged politicians in the UK from all three main political parties.

The vision for the Jubilee Centre remains, ten years on from its launch, not to simply research past and present conceptions of character – in education, professional and public life – but to shape current and future attitudes and behaviours to it. The applied nature of the Jubilee Centre's research approach allows participants at all levels to explore their own character and virtues, what they hold dear and what they do not, to allow for transformation of them – if so sought. The prime goal of the Jubilee Centre's work is practical – it is well-grounded theoretically, but allows for active transformation in how people pursue their own goals with regards living a good life. The synthesis of ideas, those brought by Jubilee Centre team, and that have been brought by others, has allowed the Jubilee Centre to demonstrate how ideas that others may previously have seen as fixed, or rooted, are much more active and freer, without any predetermined blueprint for development. In addition to the names already mentioned, the Jubilee Centre has made a deliberate and concerted effort to engage the leading scholars on character globally, bringing many to the Jubilee Centre for extended periods of time – names such as Randy Curren, Candace Vogler, Robert C. Roberts, Steve Thoma and John Haldane to name but five. Further, everyone in the Jubilee Centre has read Lickona, Berkowitz, and the other key texts from modern character and education – and Aristotle, of course! None of the Jubilee Centre's ideas, definitions, or approaches have been derived directly or uncritically from any one single source.

Breaking the ten-year history of the Jubilee Centre up into its individual phases of work – Gratitude Britain, Service Britain, Transformative Britain and Celebration Britain – is helpful when plotting the timeline and chronology. The Jubilee Journey by grant phase shows the overall focus of each grant, the timelines that each phase was bound by, and the reports that were published as part of each phase. That timeline is available on the Jubilee Centre website.[1] Aside from mapping onto the themes of the Queen's Jubilee speech, however, the four phases of grants do not hold much meaning to anyone outside of the Jubilee Centre. Particularly the 33-month time period of each grant, and with individual projects having different reporting timescales, so breaking any evaluation of the Jubilee Centre down by grant phase is only so helpful, or at least so interesting.

---

[1] See The Jubilee Journey (2020). Available at: www.jubileecentre.ac.uk/ 355/about (Accessed 1 December 2021).

The Jubilee Centre has always sought to appoint people who are invested in the idea that promoting good character is a good thing, academically and practically, and that developing character is a good aim of educational practice in and of itself. Every person who has been recruited to the Jubilee Centre has been asked a version of the question 'what is character education and why is it important to you and to the role that you are interviewing for?' In doing so, we have sought to recruit staff who are committed, who subscribe to the aims of the Jubilee Centre, and who want to contribute to the work that the Jubilee Centre is doing. Part IV of this book reflects on some of the achievements of Jubilee Centre staff in more detail, but it is worth foregrounding that since 2012 we have employed over 70 staff, from junior administrators to full professors. Many staff have been employed for fixed periods of time – as is commonplace for research-funded, higher education posts – to work on specific projects, often linked to the particular grant phase in which they joined the Jubilee Centre.

The first grant phase – Gratitude Britain 2012-2015 – was a phase of work that focussed on the foundational and theoretical conceptions of character and virtue. It ensured that the Jubilee Centre approach was philosophically sound, thus allowing more scope in subsequent grant phases to conduct research that built upon this theoretical basis and sought to address gaps in the field, or move the thinking forward even more. We spent a significant portion of time establishing our theoretical position, creating methodological approaches, and making connections – with schools, scholars and policymakers. We were, on reflection, probably most ambitious in our research projects in that first phase than in any subsequent phase – in terms of the quantity of outcomes, participant numbers, and dissemination. However, in setting stretching and lofty ambitions, so the Jubilee Centre, its staff, and its initial influence were all able to grow quickly. Establishing a research centre dedicated to character and virtues, as the only centre dedicated to the topic in the UK, required ambition and vision. It was then important to set expectations of the newly recruited staff regarding what the Jubilee Centre was established to do and what we wanted to achieve. As part of that, we incorporated lofty targets and milestones, in terms of participant numbers, outputs and outcomes. For example, both *Character Education in UK Schools* and *An Attitude for Gratitude* – both flagship projects in that first phase of research - were tasked with and achieved participant numbers of over 10,000. That made each the largest study nationally – and likely the largest studies internationally – studying character in schools and studying conceptions of gratitude. As a result, the researchers involved in each study were aware of the size of the project from the outset, so were required to devise projects that would be methodologically sound to absorb such numbers, analysis of the data was rigorous and we could make claims based on the findings that we could state with confidence.

The study that began the Jubilee Centre's work on virtues in the professions was equally bold in its approach in the Gratitude Britain phase.

Designing a study that would consider the place of virtues in both the training and practice of three major professions (medicine, teaching and law) required careful thought and planning, as well as extensive and deliberate networking to engage expert panels from the beginning, to bring greater professional expertise to the project. The work done to establish a coherent and rigorous research project across those three professions has endured and has since been replicated across four more professions (the British Army, nursing, business and finance, and the police).

The work with professions and the training of professionals has spanned a wide scope of disciplines and created significant impact both in Higher Education training, and in how regulators and membership organisations consider ethics in the workplace. The initial project brought together colleagues from varied academic backgrounds and challenged them to work in an inter-disciplinary way, whilst also establishing contacts and networks in professions that, other than education and the training of teachers, we had little immediate links with. However, as with much of the Jubilee Centre's engagement and impact, we found doors open to us that we had assumed might be closed or even locked. There is something about the language of character that, when expressed from a neo-Aristotelian perspective, and supported by a framework that foregrounds societal *and* individual flourishing, that has held the ears of most of those we have reached out to.

In addition to the three flagship research projects, we commissioned a number of smaller projects in that initial phase of work. These projects were not expected to hold the same academic rigour as the flagship projects, were developmental and practical in nature, but would supplement and compliment the initial higher profile and larger scale research led by the Jubilee Centre's team. We commissioned organisations, individual scholars, and youth workers to work on projects that were all structured around the central theme of gratitude. These projects looked at the academic nature of gratitude, and its theological links across the Abrahamic faiths; the links between charitable giving and gratitude; gratitude as a means through which to give back to one's local community through service; and the notion of neighbourliness in gratitude-centric communities. These projects supported the wider work of the Jubilee Centre, created local impact, and helped the Jubilee Centre – as a brand-new research centre – extend its research portfolio in addition to the staffed research projects that I have introduced above. We were able to work with scholars who had supported the Learning for Life work previously, and so had a grounding in what the Jubilee Centre was aiming to achieve. Further, we were able to work in local Birmingham communities, with experienced youth workers and community leaders to bring a practical focus to the Jubilee Centre's initial research. This approach of complementing and combining large scale national research with locally-focussed practical projects is one that would continue to serve the Jubilee Centre well in the coming years – in terms of creating sustained and enduring impact – particularly with school communities – and also provide a 'bottom up' approach that balances the 'top down' impact at policy and government levels.

We have strived to impact practice and policy from the outset. Creating the post of Director of Development (later Director of Education) held by Tom Harrison was a signal of this intention; that the theory and research should be applied in a transformative way. Tom's remit at first was to direct practical activities like the Programmes of Study, Thank You Film and Letter Awards, and general engagement with teachers, whilst the research projects themselves were getting underway, in terms of researchers doing extensive background reading and literature reviews, designing their methodologies and contacting schools and other participants. In addition, the Management Team set about drafting the first version of *A Framework for Character Education in Schools*. As I write this book, we are currently revising the *Framework* for a third time, and also drafting a rationale and provenance document that explains and explores both where the ideas contained in the *Framework* came from, and provides a motivation and justification for its content. This discussion of the origins and genesis of the *Framework*, as well as its impact, is important to note alongside the provenance of terms and philosophical rationale that are contained in (Jubilee Centre, 2022). The *Framework* is the Jubilee

Centre statement on character. It was conceived of as our declaration for how we saw character – what character is and what it is not. It was written for a school audience, for school leaders and governors to pick up and enact in their schools, but it needed to be academically robust as well. We published the first iteration in 2013, just over a year after the launch event at the House of Lords. To date, it has been circulated to well over 12,000 schools in the UK, as well as hundreds internationally. It forms the foundation for all Jubilee Centre research projects, how they conceive of character and virtues, and the resources and interventions that have been published along with the research. The aim was for it to be an accessible yet intelligent document for those interested in pursuing a character-led journey in their school. Whilst it has been revised and improved a number of times, the core of the original document remains – testament to the care and attention that colleagues put in to the original drafting, and also reflective of the accessible nature of it, and how schools and school leaders have adopted it. Major changes have not been required. The substantive edits were made in 2017, where the neo-Aristotelian Model of Moral Development was added, along with the Components of Virtue and an expansion of character caught and taught to include character sought – emphasising that students need to seek opportunities to develop their own character, as well as schools providing them via caught and taught approaches. These changes enhanced the theoretical side of the *Framework*, especially its focus on practical wisdom a metacognitive capacity, with changes grounded in the theoretical and practical research that the Jubilee Centre was conducting, whilst retaining the accessible and comprehensible expression of complex issues.

In addition to our work with schools, the *Framework* has formed the basis of most other Jubilee Centre engagements, particularly when speaking with businesses, charities, other organisations, and particularly scholars internationally. In many ways, the *Framework* can be said to have taken on a life of its own. Looking back on its conception, I do not think anyone in that first meeting to discuss what a *Framework* for character should contain would have believed the extent to which it has been used to facilitate meaningful engagements and create sustained impact across the wide spectrum of the Jubilee Centre's network. The *Framework* has spawned additional Statements on various topics related to character – on virtuous professional practice, on teacher education, on sport, on civic virtues, on youth social action, and specifically on the Covid-19 pandemic. The Jubilee Centre has published these Statements in response to a societal issue or challenges, or following a consultation of experts focussed on a particular theme. We published an adaptation of the *Framework* for schools in *Character Education in Universities: A Framework for Flourishing* (2020). This was developed in partnership with the Oxford Character Project, and provides a more nuanced conception of character education in universities, adjusting the Building Blocks of Character to reflect the upward direction towards flourishing students, staff and university society, as well as subtly changing the categorisation of performance virtues to performance strengths.

These changes in the Higher Education *Framework* were not reflected in the Schools *Framework* at the time, for deliberate reasons. The successes that the Jubilee Centre has achieved through its dissemination of the Schools *Framework* – with schools and in other areas – have come about through interactions, networking, presentations and sustained engagement, rather than simply posting it to schools, sharing it online and waiting for schools to adopt its principles. As such, colleagues were already articulating many of the subtle changes that were reflected in the Higher Education *Framework* when they spoke with teachers, school leaders, students and scholars. Therefore, we did not deem it necessary to change the text of the Schools *Framework* at the same time.

The Schools *Framework* has then taken on a number of different personae, including its place at the heart of how major funders consider and award grants on character. Both JTF and KFF have used our *Framework* both as a document that potential grantees should absorb and consider when approaching a funding application and as an assessment tool when they make decisions on which grants to fund. In 2021, following an extended partnership with KFF where Jubilee Centre staff had travelled to many different cities and universities across the United States to meet with and advise KFF grantees and applicants, we have delivered multiple series of online seminars on aspects of the Jubilee Centre approach to character, all of which were rooted in the *Framework*. In addition, some of the Jubilee Centre's most tangible and measurable impact has been with DfE and Ofsted in England and Wales. Much of this impact links to the *Framework*, with Ofsted adopting the Jubilee Centre's definition of character in their EIF (2019), and DfE adopting the same definition in meetings attended by James Arthur in 2014 and subsequently. I will say much more about this impact, how we set out to achieve it, and more insight into how we created it, in Part III of this book, but many of the roots of all of our impact can be traced back to the *Framework*.

Much of the influence that the Jubilee Centre has had has tended to happen around the main research projects, rather than because of a particular project, study or finding. By this, I mean that there has always been a concerted effort by the Jubilee Centre's Director, Management Team, and senior researchers to go beyond delivering the prescribed research projects in each phase of work. This approach began in the Gratitude Britain phase, the phase where the flagship research projects took most priority, and has continued through subsequent phases since 2015. That may reflect the fact that the Jubilee Centre's core leadership has not changed since 2012; James Arthur, Kristján Kristjánsson, Tom Harrison and myself remain in the Jubilee Centre, which has created settled and stable leadership and management. As such, the core aims and principles of the Jubilee Centre have not changed. The knowledge of the Jubilee Centre's history, activities, and impact and influence have remained and been retained by the leadership team, and this has helped the Jubilee Centre navigate new research phases, changes in staffing to researchers and professional staff. It has also helped the Jubilee Centre to continue to achieve its goals and ambitions, as there has remained a historical knowledge, academic understanding and administrative support for work. Retaining that leadership and management has undoubtedly benefitted the Jubilee Centre, with the shared vision and consensus of approach regards what the Jubilee Centre has done and where it is going being reflected in its achievements to date.

The four main areas of the Jubilee Centre's research portfolio were not ones that were identified at the outset, but have been reflective of the successful projects within each phase, as well as how we have continued to disseminate and engage outside of bespoke projects and in between grant phases. Planning for subsequent phases begins well in advance of the timelines of when each grant phase formally started – often as far ahead as two years before the formal start date – with an original ten-year plan outlined in the original proposal in 2012. Whilst events, research findings and changes to the academic landscape of character and virtues, and to the funding priorities of the JTF and other funders, have necessitated tweaks and rethinks of particular projects at certain times, we have stuck largely to the plan outlined in the original proposal made to JTF in 2012. Having said that, the scope and scale of our international outreach and global engagement has exceeded anything we ever documented in a bid for funding. The grant phases were designed to reflect the intended progression of research from articulating a clear theory of character, through collecting large-scale data that covered all areas of society, backed up by rigorous academic theory. Then, we moved forwards with a focus on what works in character education, the professions and society more broadly, and on to focussing on sustained character development and the transformational change that it can have at all levels. Finally, the fourth phase has become more reflective – focussing on what has gone well, identifying gaps in the literature and the practice of character, and focussing on filling them, and ensuring that character remains on the agenda with practitioners and students, and with policymakers and politicians.

The Celebration Britain grant phase will conclude the original funding agreement with JTF and the ten-year horizon vision that Dr Jack Templeton had. It will take us a little over 11 years to fulfil that vision, which probably reflects the challenges and complexities of working in the field of character and virtues and the nature of the subject matter. It has not been an easy journey! I mean that both in reference to the nature of the research and to the job of managing the Jubilee Centre from where we began to where we are on the cusp of celebrating our tenth anniversary. I was the Jubilee Centre Manager for five and a half years, and have moved on to a role directing strategy and strategic initiatives. Both roles have kept me at the heart of the activity of the Jubilee Centre, at the centre of the decision-making processes, and part of its many successes and challenges. The end of the Celebration Britain phase of work will by no means mark the end of the Jubilee Centre. The Jubilee Centre has operated with multiple funding streams throughout its existence. Whilst the JTF horizon funding has constituted the vast majority of the funding that we have secured, work with other funders has allowed us to diversify and be creative at various times. Work with KFF has created capacity for the development of a full Character Curriculum at all school ages, and secured hundreds of scholarships to study on the MA Character Education at the University of Birmingham – the world's first taught distance-learning course on character. Funding won from DfE allowed engagement with tens of subject specialist secondary teachers when developing *Teaching Character Through Subjects* (2014-2016). Additional funding from other charities such as Porticus, Templeton World Charity Foundation (TWCF) and Society for Educational Studies has complemented and supplemented the main research portfolio, as well as placing the Jubilee Centre in a very strong position for where to go post-2023.

As I have mentioned above, when the Jubilee Centre launched in May 2012, the only person 'in-post' was James Arthur. Since then, though, as people have come and gone through the Jubilee Centre, there has always been an aim to both get people to contribute within their post during their time in employment, and to help people move on to somewhere they can utilise the skills and talents that they have developed whilst in the Jubilee Centre. Of course, with over 70 employees in 10 years, from junior administrators to full professors, people have joined from a range of different backgrounds, and many who have left have moved on to a multitude of different careers. We have helped some build academic careers, study for PhDs, and others pursue other interests, become teachers, and even start their own businesses. A number have stayed beyond their initial contracts. Others have left and returned. However, only the core management team of James Arthur, Kristján Kristjánsson, Tom Harrison and myself have been in post since 2012. Danielle Edwards joined in 2013, and Andrew Peterson in 2018. The two main reasons for the management team enduring, where the research and professional teams have turned over staff in each grant phase can be summarised by saying that the leadership team have always bought into and wanted to drive forward the vision of the Jubilee Centre beyond any single grant phase. We have all invested in the ten-year horizon plan, and worked to achieve the overall aims and ambitions that we set ourselves as a centre. Whilst this may also be applicable to other colleagues, the limitations of fixed term funded posts means that we cannot offer development and promotion to every single member of the team either within or between grant phases. Generally, we have recruited early career academics and professionals who choose to move onwards and upwards to roles elsewhere in the University of Birmingham, Higher Education, or explore further study.

Those who we have employed have affected the Jubilee Centre. Their skills, knowledge, abilities and personalities have shaped the Jubilee Centre both in the day-to-day life in the office, and on how we have structured projects, built teams and recruited teams. The varied personalities, career stages, and wider academic interests have been directly responsible for the synergy and collaborations between Jubilee Centre colleagues. Some of the things we have learnt as a centre over the years have come from understanding staff experiences, trying to align expectations and objectives, and articulating the realities of working to an excellent standard, in a world-class environment. To say that the Jubilee Centre is world-class is not intended to be boastful – although we are in celebratory mood! It is a reflection on the realities of what has been achieved since 2012, how we have gotten to where we are today, and what it has taken to get there. We have made changes to how we have approached grant phases since Gratitude Britain based on the successes and challenges that we experienced in that first phase. We refined our focus on character education in schools and recruited teachers from the classroom to join our research team in phases two, three and four. We continued our work on virtues in the professions, both by broadening our remit to more professions, and, later, in recruiting a dedicated empirical researcher to analyse the data collected and to integrate analysis across the dataset. We have been innovative and creative in how we have partnered with other organisations to benefit our research portfolio. We recruited a researcher to work in the offices of Step Up to Serve on successive projects on character and service. In embedding a researcher with those leading the #iwill campaign, working closely with other campaign partners, and gaining access to young people and charity leaders for research purposes, it was possible to shape the campaign goals around character and service. Articulating and evidencing the 'double benefit' of volunteering and being of service is one of the most tangible and impactful pieces of research that we have undertaken in the Jubilee Centre.

We have always sought to recruit the people who are the best fit for the Jubilee Centre, depending on the requirements of the role. At times, this has led to a more general approach to recruiting researchers who are interested in moral theory and the practical application of character education, and has led to researchers working on projects that they bring a particular perspective to, depending on their area of expertise, within the overall Jubilee Centre approach. Sometimes, though, we have recruited specialists to work on the empirical analysis across the research portfolio, or specifically on a discrete project that advances work in a particular area, for example our current work on cyber *phronesis*. The same has been for the developmental work, where we have worked with schools across the country on practical projects such as the Thank You Film Awards (TYFA), Thank You Letter Awards (TYLA), and Jubilee Awards for Service (JAS). At times, these projects have required standard administrative support in distributing packs of materials and receiving them back from schools and youth organisations. At other times, this has required more focussed effort by colleagues to engage schools and youth groups, working closely with them to ensure submissions to programmes are of quality, and that the character development is meaningful and thoughtful, rather than transactional and surface level.

There has been a committed and concerted strategy by the Jubilee Centre to marry theory and practice across our schemes of work – to engage academic debates and engage policy and practice. A good example of this dual approach to research and development can be seen in our early work on gratitude. One of the 'Big Questions' that framed the Gratitude Britain phase was, simply, 'What are you grateful for?' In addition to undertaking the UK's largest study of gratitude, and comparing it to an existing study of US-based participants, the researchers on the project secured a small grant to undertake a cross-cultural comparison study in Australia to the UK-based dataset. This added a real richness to the study that would allow for greater application of findings and recommendations, particularly outside of the UK. The main comparison was to a pre-existing US-based study, but the additional Australian data enhanced the findings further, and expressed interesting cultural nuances. The project findings, in short that gratitude requires a benefactor, a beneficiary and a benefit in order to be expressed, have shaped the academic field, particularly with reference to Professor Robert C. Roberts, who admitted that the Jubilee Centre work on gratitude had changed his perspective. Professor Roberts was the world-leading expert on gratitude when he joined the Jubilee Centre as Professor of Ethics and Emotion Theory (2015-2017). In addition, and led by Professor David Carr, a seminar on gratitude that brought together the leading lights on the subject, held on campus in Birmingham in November 2013, stimulated discussions between philosophers, psychologists, theologians and educationalists on the importance of gratitude in public life, which was later turned into an edited collection of essays. A series of practical projects that emphasised the importance of gratitude in community work and schools. The success of the TYFA and TYLA – entered by thousands of young people from across the country – led to the creation of a Gratitude Day, where we encouraged schools and youth groups to celebrate gratitude with suggested resources and activities. Some of these have become the most engaged with activities that the Jubilee Centre produced, and bringing young people together in cinemas to watch their films on gratitude, or celebrating on campus with the display of letters that they had written to family or members of their communities helped reinforce the lived experience of valuing gratitude. We have also commissioned films that show case studies of gratitude in Britain.

As well as being an interesting virtue to study in terms of articulating the link between virtue and flourishing. The work went on to explore the theoretical and practical links between gratitude and other virtues, and gratitude has remained a central tenet to the moral conception of character. Character is a language that is used widely across society, but is a topic that people often shy away from, do not wish to discuss, or know little about. That paradox creates a 'gap' between knowledge and action, between theory and practice, something we have sought to address in our work.

2022: A Year of Celebration

Celebration Britain is the fourth, phase of the Jubilee Centre's research; so-called to follow the fourth theme of the Queen's Jubilee speech in 2012, this phase of work is intended to bring a lot of the preceding phases, findings and recommendations together, and to celebrate the place of character and virtues in British society. Celebration Britain began on 1st January 2021 and encompasses the tenth anniversary year of the Jubilee Centre. At time of writing, the Jubilee Centre has planned a portfolio of celebration events and activities that will take place across the Celebration Britain grant phase, and in 2022 in particular – of which the publication of this book will be one.

To sustain, develop and grow a research centre over such an extended period of time has taken dedication and hard work – of course – and taking time to acknowledge and recognise that, as well as celebrate with key partners and collaborators, is an important and essential part of this grant phase. The year 2022 was due to begin with our 10th annual conference, held in the familiar environment of Oriel College, Oxford, however, due to the Covid-19 pandemic, this was postponed until September 2022. This conference is our most significant of all of our conferences, seminars and public events that the Jubilee Centre has organised since 2012. I make more of those in Part III of this book, but in particular, the annual conference, or 'Oriel' as it is referred to in-house, is the Jubilee Centre's flagship event each year. We begin organising the next conference almost immediately as the previous conference ends, and we fill the delegate list every year – often with a long waiting list of delegates also wanting to attend. Where each conference is given a theme related to character and virtues, the tenth conference has been given both a wider sub-title on 'integrating research', with a specific focus on the ten years of research and impact created by the Jubilee Centre. At the 10th conference, we will convene a panel of partners that have worked with the Jubilee Centre since 2012 in both academic and practical ways, through our collaborations with UNICEF, the KFF, and academic institutions in the UK and US. This panel is in addition to the usual keynote lectures that will feature the leading scholars and policymakers working in character and virtues today.

The main event of 2022 will be the 10th anniversary event at the House of Lords in May 2022. The Jubilee Centre was launched in the Atlee Room of the House of Lords on 16th May 2012, and we will be returning to the same venue to mark the tenth anniversary. This celebration has been split into two events, a High Tea with school leaders, practitioners and other partners who 'do' character, teaching it, developing it and living it, followed by a dinner with politicians, policymakers, scholars, diplomats and other international guests. The intention behind both parts of the event is to bring together many of the partners who have worked with the Jubilee Centre to embed, advance and transform character in British society and internationally since 2012 and to celebrate the achievements of the Jubilee Centre during that period.

Something that I have learnt whilst working in the Jubilee Centre is that taking time to celebrate achievements, to stop and pause and to reflect on what has taken place or been accomplished doesn't happen all too often – in the Jubilee Centre, or in life generally. We are conditioned to move on from one event to the next, from one research project to the next, from one publication to the next, without considering the work that has gone in to making the achievement possible. Breaking up our time and work into the four grant phases has enforced periods of reflection, though, as we have had to wrap up each phase and report to JTF. As part of that, we have sought to bring together the academic and practice-orientated successes of each phase in various ways designed to be visually engaging. Such publications have been an enormous help to me when composing this book. In addition, we have always sought to secure the biggest names in the field as conference keynote speakers, to write forewords for reports, or to launch publications from the Jubilee Centre. Since 2012, such luminaries as Michael Mosley, the tv presenter and medical doctor, Dame Kelly Holmes, the Olympic champion athlete, and Sir Anthony Seldon, the educationalist, have launched publications and written for the Jubilee Centre. Successive Secretaries of State for Education have spoken at Jubilee Centre events and vocally supported the Jubilee Centre's work, including Rt. Hon. Michael Gove MP and Baroness Nicky Morgan. Leading scholars from across disciplines have collaborated with Jubilee Centre staff, given keynotes at Jubilee Centre conferences, and cited the Jubilee Centre's work such as Professors Bill Damon, James Hunter, Blaine Fowers, Marvin Berkowitz, Julia Annas. Randall Curren, David Carr, Robert C. Roberts, Candace Vogler and John Haldane have held chairs in the Jubilee Centre and stayed for extended periods to work with and mentor researchers. Many of these names and others will be present at the House of Lords in May 2022 as part of the 10th year celebrations. Celebrating the collaborations and relationships with all of these people will be as important as celebrating the successes of the Jubilee Centre.

We look forward to hosting events for specific groups within the Jubilee Centre's networks, such as for teachers and student teachers, to celebrate in different locations around Britain, such as Oxford, London, Edinburgh and Birmingham, and to expanding our networks further. We will induct more 'Ambassadors of Character Education' – celebrating leading practitioners who deliver exceptional character education provision. We will engage new audiences, via our work on virtue in the professions, character education in schools, civic virtues and the common good, and character in the digital and online space, and we will publish new research. The tenth anniversary year is a poignant and significant milestone for us to celebrate and to reflect, but it is not the end of the journey. The road continues, and we have live projects that will conclude during 2022 with new findings and new recommendations that we hope will shape the future landscape of research into character and virtues.

II

Character and Virtues
in Public Life

Introduction

I will focus in more detail on the areas of the Jubilee Centre's research via four sub-sections of research that cover character education in schools, virtues in the professions, civic virtues and social action, and gratitude and *phronesis*. This is not an exhaustive coverage of all of our research, but it covers the vast majority of work undertaken, particularly with regards the research reports and statements that we have published since 2012. Our research has built on each project that has come before it, either by expanding the scope of data collected, for example with the work with different professions, or sought to balance large empirical datasets with in-depth qualitative studies and case studies, such as with our work on character education in schools. The research has taken multi-, inter- and intra-disciplinary approaches, utilised mixed methods designs, created new measures for virtue and had impact within and beyond the academy - in schools, at policy level, with regulators, charities, youth organisations and the public. The research journey that we have been on in the Jubilee Centre has been eventful. I will talk in more detail in Parts III and IV about some of the impact, partnerships, successes and challenges that have been encountered and, here, I focus on depicting the breadth, depth, scale and scope of the Jubilee Centre's research.

For each grant phase, we have been required to submit to JTF detailed proposals that describe the intended research portfolio of projects, including recognition of the background literature and where this project would sit within it, suggested a methodological approach, and stated example outputs (e.g. reports and publications) and outcomes (i.e. our intended impact). The original research proposal submitted to JTF in 2012 sketched out a ten-year plan for research projects, projected dissemination and influence. It described movement from establishing a strong theoretical conception of character, reinforced by large-scale empirical data collection, through more rigorous and detailed focuses on particular areas of character and virtues and on to a reflective and celebratory period. In that initial plan across the ten years, we wanted to show progression. However, trying to predict the future of our academic research, three, six and nine years in advance was incredibly difficult. That made both the ambition to draft a ten-year vision and the support we received from JTF to fund us quite remarkable. Since 2012, I can say that we have sought, individually and collectively, to be remarkable. I do not say that in an egotistical sense, more so that we try to make all that we do significant and meaningful. We seek to make an impression, to bring people with us, and to create impact at all levels. We have tried to make the work that we do and the people that work with the best it possibly can be. Working in the Jubilee Centre comes with an expectation that if we seek to impact policy and practice nationally and globally, then the work that we do needs to be world-leading. In order for the work to be world-leading, so we need to adopt a world-leading approach, wanting to better what is already out there, in terms of academic research, quality of delivery, scope, breadth and depth. The expectations placed on us by funders, by the University of Birmingham and others are demanding. We expect them to be. However, we place higher expectations and demands on ourselves than anyone else does. We are more critical of ourselves, more challenging, than anyone outside of the Jubilee Centre is of us. I believe that I have set world-leading standards in my work in the Jubilee Centre and have set those standards and expectations of others that I have managed and worked with. I believe that working in the Jubilee Centre has helped me develop this attitude and commitment, stretching me to achieve more, do better, and think in different ways. This makes us remarkable.

Whenever we do take a moment to pause and reflect on what we have achieved – usually through being asked to complete an annual review form of research centre achievements, writing an Impact Case Study (ICS) for the Research Excellence Framework (REF), or some other technical or administrative requirement – we recognise the progress we have made since 2012. When the grant phases were sketched out, in a draft form at the outset, the overall journey was not prescribed. We indicated a direction in which we wanted to head, and identified potential milestones and outcomes by which we could gauge our progress and successes, even events at which we could celebrate achievements, but never marked an end. For, as character development is a lifelong process, so research into character and virtues is too. We have measured our progress, it has been informed by what has come out of the research that has been conducted, the groups, organisations and individuals that we have worked with, other ongoing work that has been conducted between and outside of the research portfolio, and with and by colleagues at different institutions globally. That work has crossed the divides between disciplines, and brought together individuals and started conversations that has usually informed the collaborations that I explore in Part III. Many of those collaborations lie within the academy. We began almost immediately in 2012 by inviting some of the leading lights in character and virtues to visit the Jubilee Centre, to work with our team and to speak at our conferences. We created a Distinguished Professors Programme and established our annual conference as statements of intent to engage, to learn, and to build networks was there from the beginning.

We did not limit that networking just to academics. We went out to visit schools, to engage teachers, too. Of course, following on from Learning for Life, as well as having already begun *My Character* and *Knightly Virtues*, we had a network of schools that were already subscribed to view that developing character was a good thing, but we needed to expand those circles, and learn from schools whom we were yet to engage and speak with. We are part of the SoE at the University of Birmingham, and a lot of us who work within the Jubilee Centre have an education background, whether having been lecturers or administrators in the SoE before joining the Jubilee Centre, or contributing to teaching and learning in the SoE whilst in the Jubilee Centre, or both! In addition, a number of colleagues have been teachers before joining the Jubilee Centre. So our focus on character education in schools came quite naturally, and built on work conducted by James Arthur, Tom Harrison and others. As outlined above, *My Character* and *Knightly Virtues* were already live in 2012, and the Learning for Life work was still being disseminated to teachers in schools, and its impact still being felt. There was far more to do, though, and far further that we could go.

Character Education in Schools

We began our research with schools, under the Jubilee Centre title, with *Character Education in UK Schools*, which would become the largest study of character with UK schools and UK school students with 10,000 participants from across the UK. It was a geographically representational study in terms of where participating schools were located and recruited from across UK, it was also representational of the proportions of different types of schools; primary/secondary, faith/non-faith, state/independent. The initial project design drew from the Learning for Life empirical work, and the construction of surveys seeking self-report data on character. However, all involved in that first schools-based project in Gratitude Britain wanted to push boundaries and see what was possible. That meant stretching ourselves in being innovative and creative in approach and methodology. It also meant reaching out to those who were working in the field to see what was 'working' in character education research, as well as liaising with schools and school leaders to understand what worked in the classroom, and whether the research and the practice were on the same page. That was some tall order in our first major research project, and there are many questions around 'what works' in character education that we are still to answer nearly ten years on, but those were the lofty goals we set ourselves at the beginning.

Such ambitions were reflected in the other flagship projects of Gratitude Britain as well, which I will come on to throughout this chapter – which looked at beginning the work on virtues in the professions, with teachers, doctors and lawyers and in an *An Attitude for Gratitude*. Both projects sought to map unchartered territories, in bringing together work on professional ethics and virtuous practice the world's largest study of gratitude, with again 10,000 respondents to the survey which drew together existing surveys, created a new measure for gratitude and had some really interesting findings that I will come on to later. However, with all projects, and the work with schools in particular, we wanted to engage schools both in the data collection for the research, but also in initial snapshots and case studies of what schools were doing in terms of character education provision. The reasons for this were multiple but can be summarised in two main aims. Firstly, as a way of keeping schools involved in research that can take 2-3 years to undertake, write up and publish is important when the aim is to impact practice and delivery. Therefore, we made a conscious effort outside of any research methodologies to work with schools to highlight the good practice and provision that was in existence. For example, we published *Schools of Character* in 2013, which showcased seven schools that were making character education a conscious part of the school day and school experience. This involved colleagues undertaking research of a different kind to recruiting participants to complete surveys or be interviewed. It was developmental in approach and allowed the academic-related members of the Jubilee Centre team to contribute to published outputs. The staffing structure that we had in place throughout Gratitude Britain separated the research from the development work, but brought academic and practical staff together, particularly on the work with schools.

Alongside the multiple school visits, administrative staff were supporting researchers in contacting schools via mailouts and phone calls to grow project participants, and to create longer-term partnerships and collaborations. One example that comes to mind was a very early visit to Wellington College in Berkshire. At the time, Sir Anthony Seldon was Headmaster, and it has existed as one of the country's most elite independent boarding schools for over 150 years. I recall a visit with James Arthur to Wellington to meet with Sir Anthony and James

O'Shaughnessy, the former Director of Policy to the Cameron government, who was working with Seldon at the time. We would go on to work in close partnership with Lord O'Shaughnessy, who is currently employed at the Jubilee Centre as a Senior Fellow, but at the time I didn't know him in an educational context, and only knew of Seldon in name, and because of his biographies of prime ministers. I went to a well-established grammar school in Sutton Coldfield, myself, and had visited independent schools during my rugby playing days, so had an idea of what to expect when arriving at the school gates. The School of Education is also across the road from one of Birmingham's most established independent schools in King Edward's School, and my office in the SoE looked out over KES and its playing fields, but I was not prepared for the rolling fields, ornate buildings and extensive grounds of Wellington. After being given a short tour of the school by James O'Shaughnessy, we sat in Seldon's office for some time, speaking at length about character and virtues, Seldon's links with positive education and mindfulness, and plans for what the Jubilee Centre could and should be doing to build a consensus amongst policymakers and practitioners for character education. Some of this is explored in both Seldon's and O'Shaughnessy's chapters in the co-authored book with James Arthur, Nicky Morgan and Julia Cleverdon *Educating for a Characterful Society* (2020). That meeting in Wellington formed the preliminary discussions both of Wellington's inclusion in the first *Schools of Character* and the Summit on character and positive education that would take place at Wellington College and Downing Street in October 2013. The Summit, a collaborative event between the Jubilee Centre, Wellington College and the International Positive Education Network (IPEN) would bring together many of the leading figures globally on character and positive education with the aims of bringing more focus to both at school and policy levels. Whilst we in the Jubilee Centre have never fully aligned the neo-Aristotelian model of moral development with the positive education approach to virtue, there were certainly mutually beneficial outcomes from both the meeting at Wellington, and the subsequent Summit.

This example shows how we in the Jubilee Centre worked in those early months to create a feeling for character in schools, engaged leading schools of character, and sought to link the academic and practical voices. We have replicated and repeated such an approach throughout the past ten years, bringing together teachers at conferences focussed on character in the classroom, the character emphasis in the revised Ofsted EIF, and establishing and supporting the Association for Character Education (ACE). ACE currently has 300 members who are at various stages of their character journeys, but whom all value character as an aim of good education. The annual ACE conference is held in a different school each year, with the event being hosted by schools that the Jubilee Centre had identified as Schools of

Character in many of the previous years. Such deliberate and meaningful partnership work was supplemented in the early phases of the Jubilee Centre's work by a dedicated development strand of work. Running in parallel to the research programmes, we created programmes that were practically engaging for teachers and students such as the TYFA, TYLA and JAS. Each of these programmes grounded the practical and educational work on character that schools and charities were delivering in the language of character that was articulated in the *Framework* and encouraged participants to apply character and virtue to their own lives, and for schools and teachers to celebrate young people for doing so. The TYFA ran for the first three years of Gratitude Britain, and combined a focus on expressing gratitude with technological engagement through amateur filmmaking. Most of the films that were shortlisted in each of the three years are still on the Jubilee Centre YouTube channel, and we brought together scores of young people to see their films on the 'big screens' of local cinemas around the country. We developed branded popcorn boxes, presented 'clapper boards' to winning classes and schools, and shared the films via our newsletter and social media platforms to showcase the articulation and appreciation that young people were giving to gratitude, as well as the people they were expressing the gratitude to. The TYLA allowed us to engage with schools in greater numbers, encouraging young people to write letters to the beneficiaries of their gratitude. Rather than in cinemas, we brought hundreds of young people together to events on campus and around the country to celebrate their letters, and had celebrity figures present awards to the young people.

The letters would appear on displays across campus in Birmingham, and we also took many into the city centre to celebrate 'World Gratitude Day' in 2014, where we engaged with hundreds of local school children, city centre workers, and members of the public on themes of gratitude and virtue. We were able, in some cases, to use the films and letters to undertake qualitative research in explorations of how young people expressed gratitude, the language they used, and who they expressed gratitude to. All of this rich data added weight to the wider focus on gratitude that the first grant phase held, and provided an additional string to the bow of *An Attitude for Gratitude*. The JAS were conceived of slightly differently, with a more direct link to the Jubilee Centre focus on service and youth social action, which began with a more developmental and practical focus, before dedicated research projects were established. The JAS, held in consecutive years at the House of Lords, celebrated public sector workers and young people for their acts of service. For many of the young people who were nominated, the JAS were a way of congratulating them for work done in their communities, for championing particular causes, and simply for showing a dedication to civic virtue in support of others. Many of the young people who were nominated for a JAS came from schools who had dedicated extra-curricular and enrichment programmes that allowed students to be of service and champion particular causes in their communities. In many cases, though, the nominees were not nominated for anything they did in school time, but for causes they championed in their own time, through charity work, or on out-of-school programmes. The intention of the JAS programme with young people was to celebrate exceptional young people for their acts of service, and, in doing so, reinforce their developing habit of service in the hope that they would continue into the future. The adult JAS celebrated public sector workers for going the 'extra mile' in their work to be of service to others. Many nominees worked in schools, hospitals, for local government, councils, the emergency services, and all were peer-nominated. In celebrating service, and in showing gratitude for each nominee's efforts, the JAS acted as an extrinsic motivator for people to continue with their lives of service. Local news media regularly picked up the good news stories of a local member of the community being celebrated at the House of Lords, and many JAS winners continued to keep in touch with us for years after the events at which they were celebrated.

The development strands of Jubilee Centre work continue, through the applied work that the teachers we have brought into the Jubilee Centre offer – such as through the development of particular resources and programmes like *Read, Grow, Go*, and in the awarding of Ambassadors of Character, which will grow a small community of character champions in 2022. It complements the research, which can often take months and years to complete, and provides real-time, tangible action and celebration of the virtues in action. The research with schools, starting with that initial large-scale empirical project in *Character Education in UK Schools*, went on to drill down on particular area of character education in schools, creating in-depth case studies, trialling different interventions and resources, before evaluating the data collected, and applying it through an online course for school leaders of character. This began with the running of multiple Massive Open Online Courses (MOOCs) on different aspects of character. Our MOOCS have been hugely successful, and have engaged in excess of 30,000 learners from across the world in short courses that foreground the key questions on character education in schools. Since then, we have developed our CPD programme 'Leading Character Education in Schools', which has had nearly 3,000 participants in two years, developing leaders of character in schools around the globe. We have created and established the MA Character Education programme that directly came out of the findings of the Jubilee Centre research. It is a practical course that provides students not only with a greater knowledge and understanding of the theories of character, but also an opportunity to design and run interventions in students' own schools to better provision for character, and an accreditation at M-Level from a leading University. The MA Character Education, along with the establishment of the University of Birmingham School, have been two of the greatest, most tangible, and, yes, remarkable outputs that we have created since 2012. I will say much more about both in the next chapter, but in relation to our work with schools, both are examples of outputs that were not conceived of in the initial grant application to JTF, but came about through developments in our work on the Jubilee Journey. In very different ways, they provide practical applications of the theoretical notion of character, and they are both world's firsts as the world's first M-Level course on character, and the first University Training School that is explicitly dedicated to character. They are two outputs that we hold very dear in the Jubilee Centre.

The research that the Jubilee Centre has conducted informs the MA course, and the course content is regularly refreshed in light of new findings, new theoretical developments, and students often engage in Jubilee Centre projects. This practical interaction with students reflects the research approach, where projects, particularly those that had an explicit focus on character education in schools, in alternative provision or in the third sector, have attempted to produce resources as additional outputs to the research. These resources then act as a give back to the institutions and organisations that we have worked with for being involved in the research, and are disseminated to similar organisations as a means through which we can engage them on matters of character. The resources are flexible and adaptable to meet the conditions and contexts of different audiences, and, in being supported by research reports that articulate what the finding are, and how they are relevant to you in your organisation, aim to be as easily accessible as possible, in order to engage as wide an audience as possible.   This approach has resulted in the creation of an Aladdin's cave of teaching resources on the Jubilee Centre's website, with resources accessed and used repeatedly in different contexts and different settings.

These resources are grounded in the Jubilee Centre's definitions, of character and of character education. These definitions were articulated early in the Jubilee Journey, and published in the first iteration of the *Framework* in 2013. They have held firm since then, and we have not changed either definition. There remains a coherence between the original *Framework* and the definitions as they have been applied in the research projects that have followed. Some semantic differences may exist, but, overall, character, character education, and each of the virtues has been defined in a consistent way throughout all of our school-based work. This has provided a consistency to our work, allowed for incoming researchers to pick up definitions and utilise them at short notice and at speed, and prevented us from 'reinventing the wheel' in every grant phase. Our work has had impact, such as with DfE and Ofsted, and our definitions have been celebrated as easy to comprehend, so there is little need to revise them for the sake of it. What has developed is the depth of understanding that supports the definitions.

Initially, we drew from other definitions and sources that were in existence at the outset of our journey, such as the Values In Actions Inventory (VIA) and other measures of character. The VIA 24 character strengths has formed the basis of a number of our research projects. It is a validated measure, and the list of character strengths provides a solid initial basis to explore character from. The VIA is a good tool for getting a snapshot of what people value in terms of their character strengths but, in terms of a neo-Aristotelian approach, there are limitations and we have been quite critical of the VIA, in spite of our use of it. For example, the VIA includes little focus on civic virtues, and it is weighted toward the positive psychology definition of character strengths and virtues, that more is better, not a virtue ethics definition of character strengths, where virtues are the golden mean between deficiency and excess.

Understanding, and then explaining, the differences between theoretical approaches to character has formed a big part of the foundational basis of the Jubilee Centre's work on character. This has not always been required in our work with schools, as teachers and students are not always interested in the differences between virtue ethics, deontology and utilitarianism. However, grounding teaching resources, the *Framework* and our wider research in accessible and clearly articulated language helps those who we engage both to understand the approach to character advocated by the Jubilee Centre, and then to see the benefits in developing good character. The Components of Virtue, and 'Caught, Taught and Sought' approaches to character have proven popular with schools. The concept of 'Virtue Literacy', holding an ability to perceive virtue, knowledge and understanding of what virtue is and an ability to reason virtuously, is another Jubilee Centre concept that schools have found easily accessible. Our work with schools has explored that, whilst also building upon the platform established by the early projects. Our early work supported the theoretical assumptions and acceptances that were already in existence, providing empirical data to back those up. For example, we found that schools that already have a rich and established character vocabulary in the curriculum, whether from a theological starting point, or through PSHE, enrichment, or other curriculum subjects, then students are likely to hold a better level of virtue literacy than schools that have little character vocabulary in use. In addition, many schools that have established character development programmes are usually developing the character of their students in a meaningful way. However, we also busted many myths that exist around the teaching of character and virtues. For example, participating in sport at school as an extracurricular activity is not necessarily a precursor to building character by itself. We have taken this to bust the myth somewhat that sport exclusively builds character, particularly because other findings suggest that students who participated in drama and choir performed better on moral dilemma testing than those that indicated that they did sport. Further, we have proven empirically that any type of school can be or become a school of character, regardless of how established their provision for character education is, and equally any type of school can perform poorly – particularly concerning moral dilemma testing. Be that primary or secondary, faith or non-faith, state or independent, a school of character is not defined by the type of school, its demographics or geographical location, but the community it serves, and how it engages its pupils. This busted the myth that many politicians perpetuated in the early months of the Jubilee Centre that state schools should learn from private schools on how to develop character, as private schools develop character best. This simply is not the case, and we have the empirical data to back this up. Whilst we were able to rank schools on their students' performance on moral dilemma testing, we have since moved away from individual character assessment as we do not see the value in ranking schools or students in terms of character. We did disprove the myth that we did not need to turn to the independent sector exclusively to learn about character education, as there were, and are, brilliant state schools developing character in a multitude of ways. The report also found that there was no systematic difference in virtue development between state and private schools. Three of the schools that participated in the project became case studies in *Schools of Virtue*, where the University of Birmingham School, Nishkam High School and St Brigid's Roman Catholic Primary School were all examined for their character provision, and the case studies reflected on the excellent character education taking place in Birmingham. Many other schools have been championed by and partnered with the Jubilee Centre – too many to mention – although our close work with Kings Langley School, the London Oratory School, Yeading Junior School and many others further shows that the type of school is not important, it is the quality of the character provision that makes a difference.

The University of Birmingham School provides a unique case study of some of the practical actualisation of building a school of character, all of which took place in parallel to establishing, launching, and developing the Jubilee Centre. As we were amassing a huge dataset of participants in the Gratitude Britain phase, and as we were engaging with policymakers at government level, James Arthur led the development of a bid to DfE from the University of Birmingham to build a school, which was to be dedicated to character. The School was opened in September 2015 by the then SoS for Education Nicky Morgan, who has been a big advocate for the Jubilee Centre and a great supporter of character education. Although she was only Secretary of State for two years, the work the Nicky Morgan did to bring character education into education policy has helped the Jubilee Centre's impact to endure. I will move on to look at policy and the continuing impact of the Jubilee Centre in part III, but it is worth referencing here, particularly about us adopting an entrepreneurial and adventurous approach to education. No one else was setting up a school at the time, no one else was doing search with 10,000 participants on character education. We were pushing the boundaries as much as possible because we believed that character education is something that should not be exclusive, should not be limited to the independent sector, to boarding schools, or only to those who have the best cultural opportunities. Those opportunities should be afforded to everyone and this has been the case at the University of Birmingham School at every level, including its recruitment strategy for staff, through its admissions policy, through the way it teaches character, through the character caught environment and through the way pupils are encouraged to seek character development opportunities on their own.

The School has gone from strength to strength, and we are proud of our relationship with it. We have taken many visitors and every member of staff who has been in the Jubilee Centre since September 2015 to the School, as well as bringing teaching and leadership staff to our conferences to speak about the unique and character-led ethos at the School. We have looked to give back to students and teachers in providing funding for extensive character development opportunities – through things like Project Wayfinder, Duke of Edinburgh Award, but also more bespoke and in-house character development. We created a film of the first sixth form to graduate from the School, which focussed on the opportunities afforded to them, and how a character-led approach has changed many of their perspectives on what resembles a flourishing life. We continue to work with the School and its staff, and celebrated Bec Tigue as our first Ambassador of Character Education in 2020. The School features prominently in many of our research projects and teaching resources – especially 'Leading Character Education in Schools'. Staff and pupils are encouraged to develop themselves and their character through additional study, trying new opportunities – particularly through the extensive enrichment programme – and in being their best at all times.

In the same light, we have encouraged staff in the Jubilee Centre to seek opportunities for development, to stretch themselves, and to push their work further. Mostly this has been through personal study, at M-Level and PhD. We have employed three graduates of our MA Character Education programme as Research Fellows in the Jubilee Centre, and engaged several others as consultants. We have engaged hundreds of schools and thousands of teachers in meaningful activities, through research projects, development programmes, conference attendance, and consultancy. The creation of ACE has strengthened the Jubilee Centre's endeavours, and whilst ACE is separate, it is guided by and immersed in Jubilee Centre teachings. ACE offers a kitemark for schools (and for charities and businesses) to reward and acknowledge excellent character provision. Such accreditation is growing in popularity, and there is a developing hub of schools nationally that truly are

Schools of Character. Creating such a groundswell of support, and of professionals and practitioners that see the benefit of teaching character will keep character on the education agenda. Another of the myths that we have busted is that character is a fad, steeped in old-fashioned, inaccessible language, and has tried to replace existing curriculum subjects such as citizenship. Such accusations have been levelled at us, although they have usually been both infrequent and easy to defend against.

We launched in 2012, as I have touched on earlier, as the Jubilee Centre for Character and Values, rather than the 'Centre for Character and Virtues'. This came from a belief at the time that the word virtue may not have been as accessible as we would want it to be in education and professional circles and that the word values was more in use, understandable and comprehensible. What we found very quickly was that the term values in schools and in professions, while very broadly understood, had a diverse number of meanings to the point that it became almost vacuous and meaningless. Schools will have a set of values, companies will have values and values statements, but that does not mean that the terms they use as values would be seen as such in the narrow virtue sense of the word. A lot of our work since 20012 has been focused on a virtue ethics approach to character and our use of the language of virtue ethics, so it made sense to rename the Jubilee Centre as the Centre for Character and Virtues. We have received very little push back from educationalists, from academics or from professionals that the word virtue is not understood. It is often championed and gets to the heart of what schools do in building the character of their pupils.

Before I move on to our work with the professions, it is worth singling out the decision in 2014 to commission Programmes Of Study for character at primary and secondary level. Since their publication, they have remained the most accessed resources on our website, viewed and downloaded hundreds of times a month by users all over the globe. They were commissioned by the Jubilee Centre, working with headteachers in the field, Geoff Smith for primary and Dan Wright for secondary, with Ian Morris and Matthew Bawden. This was our attempt at producing a full curriculum and teaching aides outlining how to teach character through all age ranges. After the *Framework* (which is our most used, disseminated and referenced document), they are the resources that we receive most interest in and requests for. Because of the generous funding of the John Templeton Foundation, we were able to print large numbers of hard copies of both Programmes, and still receive requests for them today. Our driver has never been to hit the 'magic' numbers in terms of participants or recipients, it has always been around encouraging schools, school leaders, teachers, and students to 'do' character, do it well and do it meaningfully. Rather than us just ticking a box to say that we have had 'x' number of participants compete a survey and then move on and never speak to them again.

Virtues in the Professions

Our work with the professions has been wide ranging and engaged multiple professions and several levels. Our work continues today with the current project looking at virtues in policing. It is the seventh profession that we have considered since 2012, and the sixth profession to follow an identical research methodological approach. It follows work with teachers, doctors, lawyers, nurses and business and finance students and professionals. We have also worked with the British Army, and that project took a similar approach to the other six, albeit slightly differently in some areas, and enough divergence to treat it separately.

This research was designed to deepen understanding of the place of virtues and values in initial education, training and subsequent professional practice in key professions in the UK today. The research has looked at the perceived and ideal character strengths of student and experienced professionals and their educators, as well as the levels of virtue-based reasoning applied by participants in response to moral dilemmas. Recognising that professionals work within institutional, regulatory and disciplinary frameworks, the research explored how these restrict and/or allow space for individual agency. The research has engaged first-year undergraduates embarking on their pre-service studies, final-year undergraduates coming to the end of their formative studies and professionals with at least five years of professional practice experience. The main question underpinning the work is can the professions be virtuous? In asking this, we have looked to personalise professional practice, and show how individual autonomy and professional purpose are far more important than codes of behaviour and frameworks that depersonalise and inhibit virtuous practice.

The research utilised the VIA inventory of character strengths, which were presented to participants to select their top six ideal and top six personal character strengths in their profession. Our work in integrating the findings across the first five professional studies has found congruence between career stages and between professions with how participants conceive of themselves as virtuous professionals, and what constitutes an ideal virtuous professional. For example, the virtues of honesty, fairness and kindness were the top three personal virtues across all professions, and honesty, fairness and judgement were seen as the most ideal character strengths regardless of professional differences. In spite of the criticisms of the VIA that I mention above in relation to measuring character, it has proven a highly adaptable and useable tool in our work with pre- and in-service professionals.

This work in the professions has often required us to apply our knowledge and understanding of ethics and education to a profession-specific environment, such as medical ethics, or legal ethics. Therefore, we sought to build expert panels of profession-specific educators comprised of practicing professionals and teachers of ethics in universities to advise on the construction of realistic and relevant profession-specific moral dilemmas. The findings, particularly when aggregated across the cohorts of all five professions, provide interesting reading. We can say with confidence that the moral and intellectual virtues regularly make up professionals' understandings of what character is, and how virtuous practice is identified and evidenced. Further, there are clear differences between conceptions of character amongst newly qualified and experienced in-service professionals in terms of valuing the intellectual virtues or the moral virtues, which were often supported by reference to the performance virtues. As such, we have been able to build character profiles based upon statistical analysis of the datasets collected with regards participants' ranking of moral and intellectual virtues. These groups highlight some of the fundamental differences in conceptions of character, but also the nuances between professions on how professionals live out virtuous practice and identify a sense of professional purpose. For example, we found that lawyers (solicitors and barristers) showed the lowest amount of perceived professional purpose, compared with the other five professions, and teachers, followed by nurses, showed the highest. Such a finding does not suggest that lawyers act without purpose, or indeed with a vicious sense of purpose, but that the conditions and regulatory frameworks for lawyers assume a level of virtuous practice with regards upholding the law, but may well inhibit it in reality.

Our mixed methods approach to the study of virtues in the professions has coupled large-scale empirical data with in-depth qualitative interviews. The interviews have often allowed researchers to get to the heart of some of the issues raised in the empirical data. As such, each separate project has been able to identify the key inhibitors that professionals perceive to their ability to practice virtuously – most commonly being a lack of time to reflect meaningfully on their practice, or rules and regulations preventing or limiting virtuous action. Equally, the empirical data has identified a form of inverted 'j' curve in nearly all cases, where first-year undergraduates identify virtuous reasons for navigating moral dilemmas. Such reasoning becomes much more rule-based by the time students complete their studies, and whilst some virtuous reasoning returns with in-service professions, it is never to the same extent as with first-year students. Such findings prove what the background literature suggests, that ethics modules on professional training courses both focus on rules-based ethical theories for navigating professional dilemmas, and don't provide sufficient time for students to reflect on and grapple with key ethical decision-making strategies that may affect their abilities to practice. Such findings, from a character and virtue perspective, appear to pave the way for ethics courses to adopt more virtue ethics theories in their teaching, however, our work should not appear to be so simple.

We have created good impact in certain professional quarters. Each report has been disseminated not just to universities schools and departments where professionals are trained, but also to regulatory bodies, membership organisations and the Royal Colleges that oversee professions. Reports were launched in prestigious venues, such as the Supreme Court, the Royal College of General Practitioners, and the Birmingham Council House – which is next door to the Local Education Authority building. Reports were endorsed via Forewords from some significant individuals, and launches were hosted by leading figures in each profession. However, our impact across professions has not been as successful as our work with schools and teachers. This may well be because professions hold too nuanced and unique differences that generalising approaches to professional ethics does not hold enough water for each individual profession, regulatory body, ethics tutor, etc. It may also come down to the way in which we have undertaken the work and recruited researchers to work on professional projects. Initially, the team that worked in the first phase of virtues in the professions work was not comprised of anyone with profession-specific experience, other than teaching. We did recruit a researcher with expertise in legal ethics towards the end of the project, but initially, sociologists, philosophers and a theologian staffed the project. We later recruited a practising nurse to work on the nursing ethics project, researchers with expertise in business ethics to work on the business and finance report, but few have stayed the course of each grant phase, and the management team of the Jubilee Centre has often done the heavy lifting. That is not to discredit or put down my former colleagues in any way, it is merely an observation that we have covered a huge amount of work, across a number of different areas in a relatively short period of time, much of which was semi-alien to us pre-Jubilee Centre. As such, and because of the rapid move between projects and swift turnover of research staff, the impact of the work with professions has been more about breadth than depth. That said, we have found a close partner in the Chartered Institute of Personnel and Development (CIPD). We engaged the CIPD during the Service Britain phase as a means through which we recruited practising Human Resources (HR) professionals to respond to the business and finance survey. The CIPD is a membership body for HR professionals, which has regulatory powers to act on unethical behaviours and actions. Every business has a HR department or colleague, and so it seemed a suitable and logical route to pursue in terms of recruiting participants. At the time, the Ethics Lead at the CIPD was looking to rework and revamp their ethics policies, and so the partnership had mutual benefits.

We have informed the development of the CIPD ethics code of practice and their focus on purpose. They have adopted a language of character that mirrors the Jubilee Centre *Framework*, and their Ethics Lead has contributed to Jubilee Centre consultations, publications and podcasts. This partnership is another tangible example of collaboration and impact, and how engaging a leading authority both to secure research participants and to disseminate findings and engage further, has led to some important moments in the life of the Jubilee Centre.

Civic Virtues and Social Action

Our work in the space of civic virtue and youth social action grew from partnerships that are more practical to engaging in empirical and qualitative research. Initially, in the Gratitude Britain phase, we had no research project dedicated to civic virtue. We had mapped out the development work for the JAS, and as we began to plan for the first year of those awards, the government announced a cross-party agenda to encourage young people to engage in meaningful acts of service. HRH Prince Charles, who chaired the advisory group, orchestrated this work, led by the charity Step Up to Serve. James Arthur was invited to sit on the advisory group, and attended both the launch of the #iwill campaign at Buckingham Palace, and all advisory group meetings at Clarence House. The Jubilee Centre provided academic advice and guidance to the campaign in the form of hosting an initial consultation on character development and youth social action. We recruited a researcher who we embedded in the Step Up to Serve offices in London, and who had access both to the campaign partners – comprising of some of the largest voluntary organisations in the country – and Step Up to Serve leadership. As such, this creative and innovative approach to working collaboratively has resulted in another meaningful and tangible piece of impact being achieved.

Step Up to Serve led the #iwill campaign 2013-2021, during which time we served as both its academic partner and co-founder and sponsor of the #iwill Ambassador programme. The campaign is based on the premise of getting more young people to both undertake and evidence acts of social action in their communities, with a hope that the more acts of social action a young person does, the more rewarding it becomes, and the more likely a person is to create a habit of service through their social action. Our work in this area has supported this hypothesis, and we found empirically that where a young person begins their social action journey under the age of ten then they are more than twice as likely to form a habit of service as if they begin their social action journeys in their late teenage years. This finding, from *A Habit of Service* (2017), was one that the DCMS adopted in their advocacy of young people doing more social action. Schools, too, have learned from the finding, where primary schools are encouraged to offer more opportunities for pupils to undertake social action work. Another key term that was developed from the Jubilee Centre focus on social action was the notion of the 'double benefit'. In answering the big question 'how can character be developed through youth social action?' so, the notion of a double benefit to volunteering was made more explicit. Many charities and volunteer organisations would instinctively know that volunteers' characters were being developed when they engaged in meaningful voluntary acts, but few charities prioritised the character development of volunteers over the recipients of the social action. As such, the Jubilee Centre articulation of the 'double benefit' of social action in its *Statement on Youth Social Action and Character Development* (2014) set out in writing the most effective ways for youth social action to be harnessed as a character-building activity.

Findings from empirical data gathered from surveys and interviews brought together a dataset of over 4,500 responses – the largest known study of its kind to date – found that engaging in meaningful youth social action can develop a range of virtues across the four domains of virtue. Further, those young people identified as having a habit of service were more likely to feel a sense of responsibility for their actions, and be better able to reflect on their own actions, with regards their character development. This work was undertaken in partnership with Step Up to Serve, as their campaign grew, so did the importance of character in youth social action.

Alongside the research, we helped curate an ambassadors' programme that honoured 50 young champions of social action each year. As part of the nomination process, nominees were asked to reflect on the character strengths that they thought they had developed by doing the piece of social action that they were nominated for. We found that young people were comfortable and confident in reflecting on their character development, although there tended to be a proliferation of performance virtues in the responses. I analysed the collected data from all Ambassador cohorts in an article for the Chartered College of Teaching (2020), and interviewed a selection of Ambassadors who were asked to reflect on whether their time as an #iwill Ambassador had developed their character. This work sought to close the circle on the partnership with Step Up to Serve, who closed their doors in early 2021. We were partners for seven years, recruiting six cohorts of Ambassadors, totalling 300 young people. These champions of social action stand as physical embodiments of the impact that the Jubilee Centre has had, and provide real-life examples of character development to go alongside the research.

Our partnership with Step Up to Serve led to a number of opportunities, including our partnership with SkillForce and the Prince William Award, as well as creating a new stream of research that has focussed more exclusively on civic virtue. The current Celebration Britain project *Civic Virtues Through Service to Others* draws from and extends the Jubilee Centre's work on civic virtue, service and youth social action. It is examining the meaning of civic virtue in public life in the UK. The project comes at a time in which serious concerns have been raised about several core features of democratic life, in both the UK and elsewhere. Such concerns include increased political polarisation, a deterioration in the tone of political discussion and a decline in the commitment to the common good. These concerns notwithstanding, various studies, including previous studies conducted by the Jubilee Centre, offer a more hopeful and positive picture of young people's civic commitments and engagements – including how education both builds civic character and offers opportunities for young people to express their civic character in collaboration with others.

One of the criticisms that has been levelled at the Jubilee Centre is that our conception of character is individualistic, and not focussed on any notion of community, communitarianism, civic virtue or social action. Whether it be from lack of knowledge and awareness of our civic-focussed work, or because a lot of this work began with a moral practical partnership, rather than being grounded in academic research and traditional publications, but it is an easy criticism to respond to. Our *Framework* has always focussed on individual and societal flourishing as an outcome of good character education. Our work on youth social action, and particularly work by Andrew Peterson on the links between compassion, citizenship and communitarianism have foregrounded how a civic-minded view of character emphasises the community and common good. Our publications and research portfolio support this, not as an add-on to individual character education, but as a necessary part of the holistic development of the child to seek opportunities to give back and benefit society, as well as reflect on their individual character development. This is where the meta-virtue of *phronesis* forms the lynchpin of any explicit character development. The focus on *phronesis* as the guiding virtue that conducts the orchestra of other virtues is a metaphor we use a lot in the Jubilee Centre. It helps us to discern 'what to want and what not to want when the demands of two or more virtues collide, and to integrate such demands into an acceptable course of action.' (Jubilee Centre, 2017: 4). The Jubilee Centre research portfolio has, at times, focussed on individual and selected groups of virtues, or focussed on a particular domain of virtues, and how they are expressed in public life, but has done so from a position that sees *phronesis* as forming 'part of all the other virtues; indeed it constitutes the overarching meta-virtue necessary for good character.' (*Ibid.*).

Gratitude and *Phronesis*

The reason for highlighting two virtues in isolation from our wider work on character is twofold. Firstly, we had dedicated multiple research projects, across several grant phases, to exploring theoretical constructions and public conceptions of gratitude, and the Jubilee Centre model of character education is rooted in its focus on *phronesis* as practical wisdom that guides one's ability to adjudicate wisely and practice virtuously in daily life. Each deserves special attention in their right, although our work has focussed on many others. They deserve such individual attention as they each significantly contribute to good moral character, and are more broadly noticed in public society both when they are present and when they are absent. Secondly, more so in the case of *phronesis*, which acts as a guiding meta-virtue that brings together a number of other virtues, holds multiple components, and guides our behaviours. Service is another virtue which has been singled out for special attention during the various grant phases, and which I have referenced above in the focus on youth social action.

Our first grant phase had an overt focus on the virtue of gratitude. Gratitude is a virtue that has held a dedicated research focus more than many other virtues. It is both philosophically challenging and publicly accessible, by which I mean that lay people are able to define and comprehend the concept of gratitude relatively easily, notice when it is present in society and when it is not, and has had studies dedicated to unpacking its components. One of the Big Questions that was central to the Gratitude Britain phase was 'How do British people understand gratitude and when do they think gratitude is properly experienced?' By way of answering this big question, we have used the famous Cicero quotation about gratitude being 'not only the greatest of the virtues, but the parent of all of the others.' We have used this quote in research reports, on posters on the London Underground and across campus, and in our digital engagement with students and learners. It foregrounds the importance of gratitude as a virtue, in the modern age where there is a consensus – in Britain – that gratitude, alongside virtues such as honesty;

self-control; fairness; and respect contribute to good moral character.

Our research has found that children live and learn better with good moral character and businesses operate better when prioritising and championing moral integrity. Before we began our first project on gratitude, we knew that existing research had shown a link between practising gratitude and positive well-being, amongst other positive outcomes. Our model of character and virtues does not treat each virtue as equal and equivalent to another, so with gratitude, there was scope both to explore what the public conception of it was, and also link it to other virtues, such as compassion, and to test whether a focus on one might improve knowledge and understanding of the other. Both of the two research projects that I refer to were world firsts, and in the case of *An Attitude for Gratitude*, the world's largest study of gratitude. Both studies broke new ground, and in the case of *An Attitude for Gratitude*, produced a new and robust measure for gratitude (the Multi-Component Gratitude Measure). Alongside the academic research into gratitude were practical projects that I have already referenced, the TYFA and TYLA. Whilst they were intended to be discrete projects, there was an evident overlap and each informed the other. Indeed, we produced a series of shorter research reports in the Gratitude Britain grant phase, including one which drew from the academic research being done on the larger scale project at the time and sought to apply the findings from that to the themes of gratitude that were being expressed in the TYFA.

The unique selling point of the Jubilee Centre *Framework* for character has been its focus on *phronesis*. This is both in terms of leading work on understanding and measuring *phronesis* in adolescents, and in terms of unpacking its practical application in the classroom and in public life. When we conceived of the 'Building Blocks of Character' in 2013, we made a concerted effort to present and depict each of the four domains as forming a coherent and mutually supportive whole in the pursuit of a flourishing life. To form that mutually supportive whole, there needed to be a focus on the guiding virtue of *phronesis*. Its integrative nature as a meta-virtue guides wise decision-making, and avoids a fragmented, uncritical life; or so the theory goes. The discrete research we have undertaken on exploring the facets of *phronesis* has drawn a lot from the methodological approach that was utilised on *An Attitude for Gratitude*, seeing *phronesis* as a multi-component virtue that required a multi-component measure to assess it. The work on *phronesis* across the field of character and virtues is still very much ongoing, but our work has certainly made a significant contribution. As with most projects, we have sought to engage the leading scholars on the topic, and have benefitted from the insight and contribution of others. However, the prioritisation that we have given to *phronesis* has been deliberate and intentional.

We are not claiming any scholarly ownership over the concept of *phronesis*. To do so would be absurd. What we have done in the Jubilee Centre, though, is assist in exploring and understanding the workings of *phronesis*, given the upsurge in interest in neo-Aristotelian forms of character education in the years that the Jubilee Centre has existed. We have brought the language into schools, universities and businesses – although usually via the Anglicised, less philosophical and more palatable 'practical wisdom' or 'good sense'. In addition, we have undertaken rigorous empirical work to support the theoretical conceptualisation of *phronesis* as a measurable construct and to address one of the main gaps in the research in neo-Aristotelian character education – that on the gap between moral knowledge and moral action.

That is a question we were asked many times by school and business leaders in the early days of our work – why do people still do the 'wrong' thing, when they have been taught about the importance of good character? Such a question is difficult to answer succinctly and contains many caveats and variables, but it sits at the heart of any applied work into character and virtues. To paraphrase the Aristotle quote that I used earlier, to make our work applicable to modern living in the twenty-first century, to ground theoretical concepts in real life examples, and to make exemplars and role models relevant to young people today is at the heart of bridging that theory to practice gap. Much of our work on virtue in the professions has stemmed from some sort of crisis of character in each profession where, to put it simply, professionals knew what the right thing to do was, and still did not do it. We have heard such comments from young people in schools, either made in youthful flippancy in interviews, or in teenage impatience to leave a lesson and end the school day; 'tell them what they want to hear so we can leave', or words to that effect. The gap that exists between knowing the good and doing it is hard; hard to articulate, hard to bridge and hard to measure. We are not ones to shy away from a challenge, and our work on understanding, unpacking, and comprehending *phronesis* in greater depth is something that has been a feature of our work and will continue to be moving forward.

HRH Prince William and Aidan Thompson
at the Prince William Award graduation
on 18th September 2018

Jubilee Centre teaching resources used as part of INSET
training at the University of Birmingham School
on 7th September 2015

*Aidan Thompson outside 10 Downing Street
on 24th January 2020 following a meeting
with Special Advisors for Education*

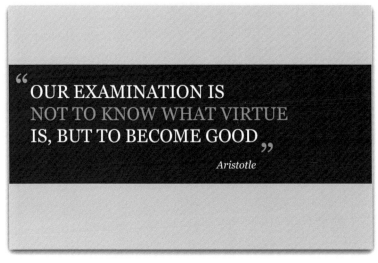

Aristotle quote used on poster campaign in 2016

*Dan Wright and Aidan Thompson at a Jubilee Centre meal
on 19th December 2017*

*Aidan Thompson speaking to young people in the UN
building in Podgorica, Montenegro on 23rd June 2015*

*Professor James Arthur and Baroness Nicky Morgan at the
opening of the University of Birmingham School
on 3rd December 2015*

III

Engagement and Impact

Introduction

Since 2012, the Jubilee Centre has created significant engagement, influence and impact in the United Kingdom and internationally – that is both within the academy and outside of it. Our research projects, the resultant publications that we have written, conference presentations and other academic dissemination have been cited widely and we have positioned ourselves as the leading academic informants on character and virtues. We have always seen our work as applied research, and therefore we have set out at every stage to disseminate findings, create influence and have impact. The academic impact of the Jubilee Centre – of those who have worked for it – has helped establish us as a global leader on character. At time of writing, we have published 40 authored and edited books, 50 chapters, over 150 journal articles, in addition to the 115 research reports, statements, *Framework* and other publications that carry the Jubilee Centre logo. Add onto that the number of blogs, resources, research summaries, briefing papers, seminar papers and other publications, and we have published 475 publications since 2012. Many of these books and articles have been cited and referenced widely across the fields of philosophy, psychology, education, sociology and others. Many have won awards and have made significant contributions to shaping current conceptions of neo-Aristotelian and virtue ethics conceptions of character and character education. On top of that, when we consider the teaching workshops, academic and practical collaborations, meetings with ministers of state and civil servants, and a whole array of dissemination strategies and activities across all of the major continents globally, we have created and, importantly, sustained impact across the academy, in practice, and at policy level.

In this chapter, I will explore the application of our research and development work in four areas. Firstly, I will reflect on the partnerships that we have created – formal and informal – with leading research centres, scholars, charities, and other organisations globally that reflect the applied nature of the Jubilee Centre and the areas we have sought to influence. Secondly, I will focus on our impact at policy level, on and with policymakers, think tanks, government ministers and civil servants – in the UK and internationally. This is evidenced by our impact on the DfE and Ofsted in England and Wales, but covers far wider reach, globally. Thirdly, our work with schools, engaging with thousands of schools around the world, forming close relationships with the best schools of character in the UK, and creating a grassroots organisation focussed on creating a network of character educators and recognising schools of character in ACE. Finally, I turn to our conferences and events, including our annual conference at Oriel College, Oxford, as well as the many other events that we have hosted and attended since 2012. These events, the annual conference in particular, are where we convene discussions between the leading thinkers in character from around the world, who come together each year to debate the most recent developments in character and virtues research.

Partnerships

I begin with partnerships, those formalised through listings on the Jubilee Centre's website, and those where we have worked collaboratively with individuals and organisations over an extended period. Originally, both in writing the original funding proposal to establish a research centre for character, and when we launched in 2012, we considered our priorities to impact the character landscape nationally. The funding proposal was geared around Britain (Gratitude Britain, Service Britain, Transformative Britain and Celebration Britain). We already had strong links with schools and organisations nationally, and the original aims were to build upon those foundations and to impact policy and practice in Britain. We saw international partnerships and collaboration as something that would develop over time, but was largely peripheral at the outset. In researching for this book, I turned back to a document that we produced in September 2013; one year after our first cohort of staff had started working in the Jubilee Centre. *Gratitude Britain: One Year On* sought to summarise progress over the first year of the Gratitude Britain grant. Even with no research projects completed, and no reports published, we had announced 11 formal partnerships, ranging from the other research centres on character around the world, to the National Liberty Museum in Philadelphia, to Wellington College. We acknowledged ourselves that despite the short period of time that had passed since the Jubilee Centre was created, that 'we have become a unique and leading centre for the examination of how character and the virtues impact on individuals and society.' (Jubilee Centre, 2013: 3). Three of the most tangible activities that we had undertaken in that first year, after recruiting a team, were to host our inaugural conference in December 2012, launch our website and monthly newsletter, and to establish partnerships with the world leading researchers on character and their centres. These the Stanford Center on Adolescence in California, the Center for Character and Citizenship in Missouri and the Center for Character and Social Responsibility at Boston University. Other early partnerships were established with Character Education Partnership in Washington, D.C (now character.org), the Character Institute who runs the VIA Inventory, the Center for the 4th and 5th R's (Respect and Responsibility) in New York, and the Center for Moral Science and Education in Japan.

Establishing key early partnerships was intended to show our ambitions, synchronise our aims, and engage with the leaders in the field. These centres are home to the world's leading scholars on character, and are – away from the Jubilee Centre – where much of the research on character and virtues happens. We have engaged other centres and individual scholars since that first year, but these were the first centres that we sought to engage with. We brought many of these leading scholars from these centres to the Jubilee Centre in the first few years as we created a Distinguished Visiting Professors Programme to complement the partnerships, and Bill Damon (Stanford) and Marvin Berkowitz (St. Louis-Missouri) gave keynote lectures at the inaugural conference in 2012. As well as reaching out to converse with the directors of such centres, we wanted, and still want, to share the latest updates, newest research findings and celebrate the successes of our peers. That is how we approached partnerships. It was an important part of our early engagement strategy to benchmark ourselves against the leaders in the field, to learn from them and engage them in our work – particularly as we sought to establish ourselves academically. Such engagement and partnership have always been conducted in a spirit of critical academic friendship, and we have also built firm collaborations, partnerships and friendships with scholars and researchers from all around the world.

In striking up formal relationships with those initial centres, others followed suit in the coming years. I referenced IPEN in Chapter Two, which James and Kristján were involved in the early stages of. This was important as it brought together thinkers from positive education and positive psychology with the Jubilee Centre focus on virtue ethics. This early partnership helped establish congruence and difference between the two fields and certainly helped clarify our academic positioning as a neo-Aristotelian centre. Such work helped establish strong foundations for the Jubilee Centre and was vital in clarifying a number of concepts on what we meant by the terms 'character' and 'character education' and how we were different from other centres and organisations. Centres such as the Aretai Centre on Virtues (Genoa, Italy) and the Institute for the study of Human Flourishing (Oklahoma) are centres that have worked with us since 2012 using a lot of the foundational work that we did to help develop their own identities, which are similarly rooted in a neo-Aristotelian conception of character. The Zentrum für Ignatianische Pädagogik (Ignatian Pedagogy) (Ludwigshafen, Germany) has consulted the Jubilee Centre on how a neo-Aristotelian conception of character and an Ignatian conception can work together. Other centres such as the Institute for Advanced Studies in Culture (University of Virginia), the Good Project (Harvard University), the Greater Good Science Center (University of California, Berkeley) and the Institute for Applied Research in Youth Development (Tufts, New York) are centres and projects that are well established and with who we have shared ideas and insights. We have visited them, they have visited us, we have co-authored papers, given keynote lectures and papers at one another's conferences, and collaborated on new research grants. The character and virtues community is one that is alive and well, one we seek to inspire and one we regularly take inspiration from.

Each partner that we have worked with, linked to on our website, is unique, and each has its own individual relationship attached to it, which has required cultivation and care. Sometimes, this has involved bringing the lead academic from a centre over to the Jubilee Centre for a week or two, hosting them, introducing them to our team, and hearing from them via our Seminar Series. This Seminar Series, in its early form, created a space and time for the leading lights in character and virtues to speak to Jubilee Centre staff and invited guests on topics close to their hearts. During the Gratitude Britain phase, visiting speakers included Lord James O'Shaughnessy, Tom Lickona, Karen Bohlin, and Marvin Berkowitz. All four of these individuals are connected to formal partners of the Jubilee Centre. In addition, we invited individuals such as Julia Annas, Hanan Alexander, Felicia Huppert, Owen Flanagan, Alex Wood and Jules Evans to give seminar papers to our team. In bringing the luminaries in the field to meet our researchers, the intention was to inspire them, so that they could better themselves in their work for the Jubilee Centre, make connections outside of it, and learn from the best around. Largely, I can say, this had the desired intention. I will say more about the seminars and conferences that we have hosted – and that we have attended – below.

In addition to the academic partnerships, we have established partnerships with leading schools and educational organisations. The first school that we partnered with was Wellington College. This was largely due to the initial connection that we established with Anthony Seldon and James O'Shaughnessy. We would also give a series of talks and exhibit our research at the *Sunday Times* Festival of Education, hosted by Wellington College, in Summer 2015. This marked a nice conclusion to the Gratitude Britain phase – which had ended in February 2015 – as we could speak to delegates about the research findings from all projects, share research reports, and engage with the students and young people in attendance. In addition to the exhibit and presentations, the Jubilee Centre sponsored the lecture given by Dr Angela Duckworth, of the University of Pennsylvania, which focussed on the performance virtue of grit. Duckworth was, and remains, a big name in character and virtues, and sponsoring her lecture gave us greater prominence to an education audience who were using the language of grit and resilience, but not always with a moral, civic, or intellectual tether. We felt it important to reman connected to the big debates in the field, but also show that partnering, sponsoring, or collaborating didn't need to mean agreeing with the conceptions of character held by others. Wellington College, Angela Duckworth, the other centres for character around the world conceive of character in their own ways, most of which differ from the Jubilee Centre notion of character, but there are usually overlaps and synergies that are vital parts of the ongoing debates in the field. Wellington College is a prominent private school in the UK, and during that Gratitude Britain phase, private schools were being trumpeted by politicians as the places that state schools could 'learn' about what character is and how it works. This is not that state schools cannot learn from independent schools, but that learning is two-way. We have championed numerous state schools of character, and we also saw many of the good things that Wellington College were doing, there character provision was well established, and so it made sense to us to collaborate with them in those early years.

Other schools that we have worked with include James O'Shaughnessy's Floreat Education multi-academy trust (MAT), and the University of Birmingham School. We formally called both partners of the Jubilee Centre due to the extent to which we worked with them to establish frameworks, curriculum and teaching materials based on Jubilee Centre definitions. The University of Birmingham School continues to go from strength-to-strength and has been celebrated nationally for its character provision. We have worked closely with many other schools, including the eight schools that feature in the CPD programme. We have not called these formal partner schools, but we have celebrated them in other ways, including inducting some of their school leaders as Ambassadors for Character, and recognising many of them for achieving the ACE Kitemark for character provision. In addition to the schools that we have worked with, we have formed bespoke and individual partnerships with a number of other organisations.

The #iwill campaign began in 2013 and was run by Step Up to Serve until 2021. We worked very closely with Step Up to Serve during that period to undertake research on service, social action and character – embedding a researcher in the Step Up to Serve offices in London, and creating and funding the first six cohorts of #iwill Ambassadors, young champions of social action. We acted as the academic partner to Step Up to Serve, giving their work some academic credibility and gravitas. At a policy level, this included James sitting on the #iwill Campaign Advisory Council, chaired by HRH The Prince of Wales. James, and others, kept character on the social action agenda as a positive outcome in and of its own right, alongside the benefits associated with doing volunteer work. Collaborating with Step Up to Serve also helped us gain access to some of the biggest charities in Britain, their staff and young people, to participate in research. Again, this worked to keep character part of the conversation at an organisational level, with charities using a lot of virtue language in their external communications and online, but not necessarily always living it in practice. Working with such organisations helped them refocus on the importance of character development as being central to what they do and as part of their organisational aims and missions. Collaborating with Step up to Serve was mutually beneficial, and led to a focus on service, social action and the civic virtues which we had begun through our developmental work in the earlier grant phases. The synergy between the research that we conducted and the celebrations of young people and public sector workers for their acts of service serves as an important case study for how applied research can work to impact academic, practice and policy audiences. It also provided a form of model for how we might work with other third sector organisations and charities, providing academic expertise through applied research.

We also collaborated with the National Liberty Museum (NLM) in Philadelphia. That partnership entailed becoming the NLM's academic partner where we received a small grant from the NLM to undertake an additional research project, titled *Torchbearers of Liberty*. The project funded an additional researcher in the Jubilee Centre, as well as a researcher based in the NLM, and examined the NLM's approach to character and civic education through the lens of liberty. The unique project and collaboration served mutual benefits, with the Jubilee Centre providing an academic grounding and methodological basis to the research, and the NLM showing the practical display and application of an educational resource in its exhibitions. I was fortunate to visit the NLM a couple of times during the project and for its launch in 2016. I remember going for a jog to the 'Rocky Steps' in Philadelphia in sub-zero conditions before attending a series of launch events and activities at the NLM, as well as the Union League Club, where Jack and Pina Templeton were members. The JTF have their head offices in Philadelphia, and there was an established link between JTF and NLM – which is largely how the collaboration on *Torchbearers of Liberty* came about; they recommended we become the academic partner on the project.

Our partnerships with third sector and more practice-focussed organisations have always had an ultimate aim or goal, largely centred on affecting curriculum and/or educational practice, with regards a character focus. Charities, educational bodies, campaigns, and other organisations contact us on an almost daily basis, asking us to provide both an academic basis for their work, and regularly to adopt our character *Framework*. We have learnt to be more discerning regards who we engage and for what purpose, as to speak with everyone that contacts us would simply be a full-time job in itself. However, we have also always tried to engage with anyone that reaches out. Often that has simply been to signpost a piece of research, teaching resource, or other publication on our website, but it has also extended to full partnerships such as the ones introduced above. In addition to Step Up to Serve and the NLM, it seems appropriate here to reference our partnership with the educational charity SkillForce. Founded in the late 1990's, SkillForce was a charity that utilised ex-Service instructors to deliver character-led programmes to young people in schools around the country. They approached us in 2016 regarding some initial consultancy work to establish a new programme akin to the Duke of Edinburgh Award, but for primary-aged pupils. Prince William was the charity patron, and SkillForce wanted to show how a Prince William

Award (PWA) could engage younger pupils and primary schools in what they referred to as 'confidence, resilience and self-esteem'. On working with SkillForce, though, we were able to affect their thinking to reconceive the PWA as a character-based award; with the three performance virtues that they had identified having roots in other intellectual, moral and civic virtues. The PWA launched in 2016 and in 2018, the first cohort of pupils were due to 'graduate' the PWA, so we offered to host an event in the Great Hall at the University of Birmingham for pupils, teachers and parents to come and celebrate their achievements. On 18th September 2018, having spent many, many hours planning, administering and facilitating arrangements for the event, we welcomed Prince William to campus, and I was fortunate enough to be formally introduced to him.

The above section has attempted to convey some of the rationale that the Jubilee Centre has employed in our approach to creating meaningful partnerships. The partnerships reflect the extensive networks that we have created at practitioner, scholarly and policy levels. We have worked hard to establish and maintain our partnerships, and the number, depth and quality of partnerships overall has only grown in the past decade. That is reflective of both the efforts that we have put into cultivating them, and the reciprocation that we have received from peers. At times, our partnerships have led to more energised engagement at school and community levels, or at policy levels, and at times, we have been challenged in our academic work to go further and go deeper. Not all of our partnerships have been formalised in placing logos and reciprocal links on our website, but they have been a treasured part of our journey to date. Since I became Director of Strategic Initiatives in late 2017, I have overseen, managed and developed new and existing partnerships. I have enjoyed immensely the variety and quality of conversations and collaborations that I have had. These have taken me to places that I never would have visited, met dignitaries from many areas of public life, and undertaken work that has helped move the character agenda forward.

Policy

We in the Jubilee Centre are very proud of the impact that we have created on English education policy. From inviting Nicky Morgan to give her maiden speech as SoS for Education in Birmingham in 2014, to Jubilee Centre definitions of character being adopted by DfE and Ofsted, the impact has been significant. Our research findings and *Framework* are cited in policy documents, and DfE made character the fifth stated aim of the department, which it remains as today. Ofsted prioritised character in their EIF (2019) under 'Personal Development'. The Ofsted definition of character is almost identical to the Jubilee Centre definition. We know, through the conversations that we held with Ofsted colleagues that led to the EIF revisions that they felt that our definition covered the approach to character that they saw was best, so saw no reason to redefine character in any other terms. The result of this top-down impact at government policy level has meant that thousands of schools across the country are now formalising provision for character education in ways that they had not done so before. Much of this provision is meaningful and intentional, as in doing so school leaders have seen the positive value in prioritising character education.

DfE released a framework on character education for schools in late 2019, shortly after the Ofsted EIF had been implemented. This guidance cited Jubilee Centre research and signposted us as an organisation that 'support character education and development in children and young people.' (DfE, 2019: 12). Many of the other organisations named in the document are organisations that we have worked with, advised, evaluated or collaborated with, showing that the network of character educators in the UK is both diverse and varied, and inter-connected and supportive of one another. There have been six SoS for Education during the lifespan of the Jubilee Centre. Each SoS has placed a different public emphasis on character, the fact that character has remained part of the educational discourse at policy level reflects the depth of impact that we have created. Whilst her predecessor Michael Gove was interested in character, and approved the DfE funding for the University of Birmingham School, it was under Nicky Morgan's tenure (2014-2016) that DfE formalised their commitment to character education in schools. Of the SoS for Education that have held office during the

Jubilee Centre's lifespan, Morgan has been the biggest and loudest advocate for character education. We secured her maiden speech as SoS in 2014 when she came to Birmingham to give the annual Priestley Lecture for the School of Education, at which she acknowledged Jubilee Centre research as having informed her thinking on character. Since then, in addition to the meetings with civil servants and citations in policy documents, in Hansard, and in speeches, Morgan has opened the University of Birmingham School, given the after-dinner speech at Oriel in 2020, and co-written a book on character with James Arthur and other distinguished names from education policy.

We have also brought politicians to campus, sometimes for meetings in the Jubilee Centre, and for events where significant figures have spoken at celebratory events, panel discussions, and open public forums. We hosted two 'Character Matters' events in 2015 and 2016 where we assembled panels of well-known public figures who spoke about their understanding of character and how it had helped them succeed in their lives. The second of these events had a line-up of current and former SoS for Education or shadow SoS for Education, with Michael Gove, Nicky Morgan, Tristram Hunt and Estelle Morris. We opened this event to staff and students and expected all of the speakers to be given a hard time during the Q&A, particularly Michael Gove, given the public opinion of him during his time in Education. However, the event was a huge success, with Gove admitting that whilst he valued the focus on character education privately, he could and should have done more to make it explicit, as Morgan subsequently did. The first Character Matters event had brought David Blunkett (another former SoS) to campus, along with Kelly Holmes, Robert Winston and John Sergeant, each of whom spoke about their careers and why a focus on character is important in professional and public life. We invited the speakers to join us for a dinner after the event by way of expressing our gratitude, and I was tasked with dragging Kelly Holmes away from the many students who wanted to ask her questions and grab selfies, and walk her across campus to where the dinner was being held. I am a keen amateur runner and found myself incredibly star struck to be speaking with a double Olympic champion. I remember shouting at the television as Kelly went from back to front to win the 800m and 1500m in 2004. I would later get Kelly via her Dame Kelly Holmes Trust to write the Foreword to *Flourishing From the Margins*.

We have also influenced education policy aboard, having met ministers, civil servants and other policymakers in Colombia, Iceland, Japan, Malaysia, Poland, Slovenia, Saudi Arabia and other countries. Most of these examples have been initiated by civil servants in the country in question, rather than sought out as opportunities for dissemination and impact by the Jubilee Centre. As I have already said in this book, the global engagement of the Jubilee Centre has been our biggest strength, but also our most surprising, as it was not something that we had necessarily targeted ourselves. That said, we have sought to engage with those that approach us in an open and positive way. We have needed to be judicious with regards what constitutes a good use of our time, resource and capacity, as well as whether or not somewhere is a nice place to visit! One such approach that we received in 2013 was from Ben Perks, Head of Campaigns and Advocacy at UNICEF. At the time, Ben was Representative to Montenegro, and had come across the Jubilee Centre's work and wanted to reach out. I recall meeting with Ben in James Arthur's Head of School office in the SoE, and Ben set out his vision for wanting to bring a character focus to Montenegro and asked if we could support him. I have to admit, I did go away and look up exactly where Montenegro was on a map, as we agreed to collaborate.

Myself and colleagues have travelled to Podgorica and Skopje multiple times, and spoken in schools to young people, presented to teachers at major national conferences, and drank wine at the British Ambassador's house. The partnership with UNICEF has also taken us to Geneva and to New York. We have struck up a genuine friendship with Ben, and he has put huge effort in to bringing a character focus to education in Montenegro and North Macedonia. We have reciprocated by making Ben an Honorary Senior Fellow of the Jubilee Centre, and by bringing UNICEF colleagues, government ministers and practitioners in Montenegro and North Macedonia to Birmingham and taking them to visit local schools, to meet with Jubilee Centre colleagues, and enjoy a traditional Brummie Balti. I am privileged to have played a part in affecting the education policy and practice in Montenegro and North Macedonia, and it is a partnership that is greatly valued amongst colleagues in the Jubilee Centre.

Schools

I have already reflected considerably on our work with and in schools earlier in this book, so I will take the opportunity, here, to say more about some of the particular outputs that we have published that showcase the superb and inspiring practice that takes place all over the country. I am continually inspired and impressed with the enthusiasm, expertise and grace that the teachers we meet and engage with show, both to us and in their practice. My parents were both successful primary head teachers in Birmingham, and whilst they did not name the term 'character education', I know that they were great character educators and role models. Through the work of the Jubilee Centre, it has been both an honour and an important mission to support teachers to be the best character educators that they can be, by undertaking research that recommends improvements to character provision and practice, and by developing teaching resources that can aide delivery in the classroom. That then can only positively affect the young people in their care, with regards their own character development, and then positively influence their own life chances, personal development and roles as good citizens. Our work has not been contained to mainstream schools, either, as we have sought to engage tutors and young people in alternative provision, youth work, social action and volunteering, mentoring organisations, football academies and many other modes of education. We have engaged students and lecturers at university-level and have engaged professionals in practice across a range of sectors. We have even produced teaching resources for young offenders in prisons and had preliminary conversations with Arsenal Football Club about engaging their first team on matters of character.

I worked on a film that we called LEAVERS for the University of Birmingham School in 2017. That summer marked the graduation of the first sixth form from the School. We in the Jubilee Centre wanted to mark the occasion and give something back to those students who had put their trust in the School to come and study for their A-Levels. We worked with the University's film crew to capture as many voices of sixth form students as possible, asking them to reflect on how the School has helped shape their character. We then gave a copy of the film to each student as a leaving gift. The film captures the student voice of that year group really well, and shows both the students and the school on a developing character journey. Another publication that I think helps capture the spirit of our involvement with schools was *Windows Into Schools: Celebrating Character* that I co-authored with Michael Fullard and Danielle Edwards. The publication highlights the diverse practices the schools adopt in their character provision. The publication compliments the online CPD programme that Michael created with Paul Watts in 2020. It aims to bring to life the reasons why we celebrate each school and brings together the eight schools for readers to see that there really is no blueprint for doing character, but that regardless of what you do, it is essential to do it in a meaningful and authentic way.

One of the main outcomes of character education in schools linked to our work has been the creation of ACE. To supplement the policy-level engagements that we were seeking, we wanted to build up grassroots support by bringing teachers and school leaders together as a collective, to share good practice, learn from one another, but also create a force for change. The initial meetings to establish ACE were hosted and facilitated by the Jubilee Centre and James and Tom are founding trustees. Tom has been Secretary since its formation. ACE currently has over 300 members. We continue to work closely and supportively with ACE in a multitude of ways, including sharing findings, supporting one another's conferences and events and providing funding where needed. One thing that ACE offers is its Schools of Character Kitemark. The Kitemark is a mark of recognition for the provision that a school (or business or charity) have dedicated to character. When the Jubilee Centre created ACE, one of the things that we were being regularly asked by schools was for to provide an endorsement of their character provision.

We have never been set up to be able to do that, however, so we passed that objective over to ACE when they were created. We have spent years in trying to find the best ways to 'measure' character, and have set aside much of the contentiousness around measuring character by focussing largely on evaluation rather than measurement. ACE's Kitemark does this, using the Jubilee Centre *Evaluation Handbook* as its basis, by evaluating school approaches to character caught, character taught, planned and reflective approaches and interaction with the local school community. Currently, over 50 schools have been awarded the Kitemark, in addition to charities and businesses who deliver character programmes. The ACE annual conference brings together members and is hosted in one of the member schools each year. The conference presents big name keynote speakers from across education policy and practice as well as offering workshops run by experienced character educators for members to participate in and enhance their understanding of character and abilities to practice virtuously. ACE offer a practical conference that differs very much from the conferences that the Jubilee Centre runs, although they complement one another a great deal. The Jubilee Centre has hosted 20 major conferences and many more seminars and community events. Whilst there has tended to be a practice-focus to some part of each, none mirror the ACE conference in its format.

We have found that our conferences and events have enhanced our research and impact in both traditional academic channels and with the wider community of character. Our annual conference at Oriel College, along with our less frequent summer conferences have brought the academic community together to discuss matters of character. In addition, the many, many workshops, seminars, one day events, community events, school presentations, residential events have engaged an enormous number of people from schools, charities, youth work, parents, school students, pre- and in-service professionals, policymakers, and many others.

Conferences

I have never enjoyed event organisation. I find it stressful, as on the one hand you are in total control of every detail, whilst on the other hand totally at the behest of delegates to provide abstracts, papers, dietary requirements, accommodation requests and any other information that you need from them. Academics, too, are invariably late to respond to most things, which pinches the amount of time you leave yourself to 'do the admin' around a conference or event. It is a small wonder, then, that I have managed or administered some 15 international conferences and at least 20 seminars and smaller events. Whilst I do not enjoy the event management, it has been a major part of my life in the Jubilee Centre, so I have tried to find some pleasure in it. This has usually found its form at the bar during the conference or asleep on my sofa once home afterwards. Most of my dislike of conference organisation comes from setting very high standards of myself and for the event, and then being concerned that something outside of my control will lead to the event not meeting those expectations and standards. Having said that, I am very proud of the conferences that the Jubilee Centre has hosted since 2012.

There is a saying that I came up with to set expectations of professional staff in the Jubilee Centre that 'we have never done a bad event'. This is true; we never have. At least, I do not think we have. Every event that the Jubilee Centre has hosted has run on time, been well administered, and been academically excellent. Of course, there have been issues at each, too many of which remain engrained in my brain, but we have not let the quality of the event suffer as a result. I have used a metaphor that is that professional staff in the Jubilee Centre should be the feet kicking frantically under the water, whilst James, Kristján and others are the swans gliding serenely over the surface. In short, get done what we need to get done, but don't make a splash whilst you do it. This has generally worked, as I can think of only very few isolated moments at conferences where anyone other than the conference organisers have known about a particular drama or issue. There has also been wine. Lots of wine. James encourages alcohol consumption every year at Oriel, partly to break down social barriers and get delegates speaking to one another more freely, and so that they do not focus on the student accommodation that they sleep in! I have learnt more about wines that I could have imagined working for

James, to a point where he trusts me to select them for dinners and events without needing his confirmation. I knew the first time that happened that I must have been doing at least one thing right! The reason for encouraging the socialisation is that, in short, we try to get our delegates to enjoy their time at our events. That comes, in part, from a belief that the most important work at a conference is done outside of the keynote and seminar paper presentations and from experience of having collectively attended far too many conferences that are dull, not overly social, so that one ends up disengaging. We value our delegates, and the time that they have given to attend our conferences. That is particularly the case with Oriel, which takes place in early January, so delegates regularly fly from overseas on or just after New Year, reducing time spent with family or friends over the festive period.

In all seriousness, though, our events have really enhanced our public profile in the Jubilee Centre. They have brought together delegates from different backgrounds, countries and disciplines and we treat everyone as part of the Jubilee family for the duration of the conference. From our inaugural conference in December 2012 to our tenth conference at Oriel in September 2022, we have had 1,005 delegates attend our annual conferences. This only averages at around 100 per event, but that is because we limit attendance each year by paper submission or invitation due to capacities in the lecture theatre and the dining hall, and it also includes our 2021 annual conference that we were determined to run in-person during the Covid-19 pandemic. As such, the event has become a hot ticket to hold each year. We have established a community of delegates that attend every year, all of whom contribute to the collegial and convivial atmosphere at Oriel. We change the theme each year so that we can balance the return of familiar faces with new ones, but that has tended to increase the numbers of familiar faces, as well as leave more people disappointed each year as demand to return increases. It is hard to describe the significance that Oriel has taken on, as the physical event in our calendar that epitomises a lot of the work of the Jubilee Centre, the Jubilee Centre approach to engagement and networking and socialisation. It is probably apt to say that the Jubilee Centre would not have been as successful as it has been had we not established our annual conference as a signature event in the calendar. It can sometimes be the lightning rod that conducts multiple bolts of academic thought, the place which conversations begin that turn into research grant opportunities, scholarly collaborations, or simply the sharing of current theories, research and practice on character and virtues.

Our inaugural conference took place in December 2012. It stands alone from the other nine conferences in its timing, pre-Christmas as opposed to immediately after New Year, as a two-day conference, not three, as the only annual conference to take place in Birmingham and its format with the parallel sessions taking place on day one, and the keynote lectures taking place on day two. We also used the conference to launch our website and monthly newsletter. So, not too much pressure to heap on a team who had only been in post for three months and were operating without a full administrative make-up. We opened a call for papers, solicited some from friends and colleagues from the field of character and virtues, and secured some big names in the field as keynote speakers. Looking back, this was probably the most remarkable achievement of the first sixth months of the grant. The launch was a great beginning; the recruitment and selection of the team was a feat of endurance; building the website from scratch was nerve-wracking and a step somewhat into the unknown; but it was that first conference that was the biggest success of those first few months. To bring together leading names including Marvin Berkowitz, Bill Damon, Howard Gardner and James Hunter, as well as seminar papers by the likes of David Carr, John Haldane, Anthony O'Hear, Kevin Ryan, and a whole variety of other early career academics and practitioners was amazing. Everyone we contacted wanted to attend and to speak. Many of the speakers knew each other and knew of one another's work, but everyone said that they had not all been in the same place at the same conference before. Looking back, to achieve something that no one else had, with our first conference, is somewhat remarkable. Prior to the Jubilee Centre, the field of character and virtues research, while small, was also very fragmented. One of the main achievements of our conferences is to have united the field. We have invited all of the major players in the field to give keynote addresses at our conference – most of whom have accepted and delivered. We created that first conference at a moment's notice, and managed to secure the biggest names in the field to attend and speak. That first conference set the benchmark for all future conferences that we have hosted.

The inaugural conference was held on 14th and 15th December 2012 in the run up to Christmas. At the time, it asked a lot of our young team to focus their energies on such a significant event as term was winding down. We all certainly enjoyed Christmas that year, and the time off that we all took. We moved the conference to January from 2014, and to Oriel College, Oxford. James is an alumnus of Oriel, having completed his D.Phil there, and they welcomed us warmly. It meant moving the conference to early January, rather than mid-December, but the location, set up and character of Oriel make it a special place to host conferences. We intended to move to Oriel for one year, but as the refurbishments in Birmingham did not finish until 2018, we have stayed at Oriel and not returned. It would be strange, now, to leave Oriel and we have recently announced the theme for the 2023 conference.

Many of the most memorable moments from Oriel take place away from the keynotes and seminar papers. That is not to say that the papers have not been top drawer; they have. Most sets of conference proceedings have been published as either the special issue of a journal, or an edited collection. What I mean is that the academic standard of the conference has been established, but the Oriel conferences have been built on the social engagements. The drinks receptions pre-conference dinners usually held in the Champneys Room are nice opportunities to ensure that delegates begin to relax and enjoy themselves. Moving the conference to September in 2021, because of the pandemic, allowed the drinks to move onto the lawn in the College quad. We had a mini Indian summer that year, which added an additional element to the conference atmosphere as we drank a glass of fizz the sun went down. Other memorable moments include the conference entertainment, particularly when James asked our conference administrator Fiona to give an operatic vocal performance one year, giving her only a few minutes notice to agree and to warm up. Fiona agreed and gave a fabulous performance, made even more remarkable considering she had only been in post for a month. She was invited back the following year to perform with her group, too! James likes to ask his team to go further than the extra mile, but he does so trusting that they are capable of exceeding expectations. He did the same to me in 2021, asking me to give the after dinner speech. As James said on introducing me, I got twenty minutes to prepare something when other speakers usually get a year. I managed to say something fairly coherent, meaningful and amusing and it was an honour to get to do.

Whilst we moved the annual conference away from Birmingham to Oriel College, we have kept a presence on campus with other major conferences and events. These have included a major symposium on gratitude (2013), major international conferences on virtues in the professions (2016) and character in the arts (2018), and a major one-day conference for teachers on implementing the new Ofsted Framework (2019). These are in addition to over 100 seminars given by Jubilee Centre colleagues and visitors. I have been involved in the organisation of nearly every event that the Jubilee Centre has hosted, but was most involved in the 2018 conference 'Educating Character through the Arts', working with Professor David Carr to bring some of the world's leading scholars on the arts, character and aesthetics to Birmingham. This conference remains special to me for a number of reasons. Firstly, because it is a particular area of focus in my academic studies, both as an English graduate and through my doctoral studies. Secondly, that it created an opportunity to work closely with David Carr, a person who I have huge respect for and enjoying working alongside in the Jubilee Centre. Thirdly, that it was the conference at which I gave my first formal presentation; and fourthly, as I have since led a project to publish the conference proceedings, and is under contract with Routledge. That is in addition to getting to spend time with such luminaries as Noel Carroll and James O. Young, as well as meet my, now, PhD supervisor Laura D'Olimpio for the first time. It also marks the only conference that I have either organised or attended where we could not contact the keynote speaker just before he was due to present his paper. Where I say that the Jubilee Centre has never done a bad event, we almost tripped up where James O. Young had overslept through jetlag and arrived to give his keynote by sprinting down the aisle of the lecture theatre, hair still slick from a shower, some 15 minutes after he was due to have started speaking. Thankfully, no real harm was done and we all found amusement in it. This is what I mean, though, when I say that I do not enjoy event organisation as something completely outside of our control nearly led to some embarrassment.

I do not intend to reflect on every event that we have held since 2012, but will conclude this chapter with a few final remarks on some other memorable moments from across the academic conferences and the public engagement activities that we have undertaken since 2012. In addition to meeting Dame Kelly Holmes at the Character Matters event in 2015, we have also had other Olympic champions come to Jubilee Centre events, including Greg Rutherford (also 2015) and Dame Katherine Grainger (2013). Both spoke openly about some of the qualities of character that have helped them on their journeys to becoming Olympic gold medallists. Often sports people prioritise the performance virtues, such as perseverance, resilience and self-discipline, but both spoke about the moral and civic virtues that have helped them, particularly about how grateful they are to the people who have supported them. We have also worked with United Academy 92 (UA92), which was founded by the Class of '92 Manchester United players including Gary Neville. Neville is an advocate of good character development and UA92 have a bespoke character development programme for their students. I convened a consultation at Windsor Castle in 2019 that looked at character and sport, and we brought together some of the leading organisations, scholars and teachers to discuss the type of character that sport builds. Being able to include 'Windsor Castle' in your invitation to people definitely offers something to help persuade very busy people to make time to engage with you. At that particular consultation, we brought together representatives from Premiership Rugby, the Premier League, the Invictus Games, Sports Leaders, as well as many leading universities. Michael Fullard and I chaired the consultation, and it resulted in the publication of the *Statement on Character and Sport*. That *Statement* joins the suite of other statements that the Jubilee Centre has published, usually written following similar consultations at Windsor Castle. Character and sport are interesting bedfellows, and I certainly think there is scope to go further, both in research terms and in influencing policy and practice at all levels. I chaired an ESRC-funded event in November 2021 called 'Sport for a New Generation', which brought together speakers from academia, charity and the mainstream media. Whilst each speaker spoke from seemingly disparate and different perspectives, when viewed through a lens of character there is huge overlap and congruence between themes such as motivation, rehabilitation, business, social cohesion and equality. It is a hope of mine that we in the Jubilee Centre will do more in the area of character and sport in the future.

Three other memorable moments stand out to me when I think back across the past ten years, about events and conferences. I have been fortunate to attend at least seven consultations at Windsor Castle since 2010 when I began working for James Arthur. The one that stands out the most was one that took place before the Jubilee Centre was created, but is a story worth telling. All of our consultations take place in St. George's House, the venue that was established by the Duke of Edinburgh to bring together people from across society to 'effect change for the better in our society by nurturing wisdom through dialogue'. St. George's hosts many consultations on many different themes, and I can say that it is always a privilege and an honour to spend time there, not simply because of the venue, but also the ethos of the House, which is built on 'openness, honesty, trust and respect'. I do not mean to betray the rules and culture of St. George's House in telling this anecdote, but it is something that we remind our guests of each time we return. St. George's House operates an honesty bar, which opens after dinner each evening. The prices of drinks are listed, and a moneybox is present on the side for people to pay their way into. Consultations are usually two-day, with an overnight stay. The lounge area where the bar is situated is very cosy and quite intimate – it is a house after all. It is very conducive to facilitating both social and professional conversations amongst delegates. The particular consultation that I am recalling must have taken place in 2011 or 2012. I will keep this account anonymous, so as not to embarrass anyone personally, but we enjoyed our evening. We were packing up to leave the following day when James and I were called back by St. George's House staff. We assumed that either we had left something behind, or they were asking if we had enjoyed the stay, but there was a look of both alarm and embarrassment on their faces as they told us that the honesty bar had been left £60 short of the drink that had been consumed. I point out that this was at a consultation on character, at a venue that promotes honesty and trust! We, naturally, were as embarrassed as the staff at St. George's House and covered the shortfall, but it has become an anecdote that we tell to delegates at subsequent consultations.

One area linked to conferences and events that I have not highlighted is the amount of foreign travel that we do as a centre. I have been fortunate to visit many places around Europe and North America through the Jubilee Centre, and colleagues have travelled to virtually every continent to speak at conferences, meet ministers and civil servants and to teach. In addition to the wonderful memories that I have of visiting Podgorica and Skopje with UNICEF, I have most enjoyed my trips to the United States. We have covered much of mainland USA with our engagement, and one series of events in 2018 took some members of the Jubilee Centre literally from East coast to West coast, with visits and engagements in New York, Philadelphia, Phoenix, Los Angeles and San Francisco over the course of ten days. I joined that trip in Phoenix, flying in by myself and meeting colleagues to go to Mary Lou Fulton's Teachers College at Arizona State University. After that, we were due in Los Angeles, before flying up to San Francisco before flying home. Even after many years of both travelling to the USA and of working for James Arthur, I remain naive on occasion, in this instance of the distance between Phoenix and Los Angeles and the time it would take to travel. Of course, an internal flight seemed the quickest, but James suggested to me that it might be a nice change to drive from Arizona to California, particularly in light of the number of internal flights he and other colleagues had already taken on the trip. I need little encouragement to drive when abroad, so I was very keen to oblige. We hired a car – I say car, it was a huge Chevrolet SUV – and had intended to leave ASU by mid-afternoon to beat rush hour traffic. We had an initial set back on our itinerary in getting to the hire car company and then signing out the car. We were now departing right in the middle of rush hour and what had been planned as a jovial and 'fun' drive through the desert had already begun under some tensions. We found a suitably appropriate country music radio station to listen to, though, and set off. The drive was generally fine – barren and repetitive, but still fine – and we agreed to stop for an evening meal when we neared Palm Springs. We enjoyed a pleasant meal, followed by frozen yoghurt (a typical dessert of choice on Jubilee Centre away trips). My colleagues enjoyed a bottle of wine with dinner and I specifically asked if they would stay awake when we got back on the road, as we would be approaching Los Angeles in darkness and we had taken enough wrong turns already for me to want to navigate the final leg solo. I also wanted the company of being able to talk when driving at night to keep myself alert. They all agreed to stay awake – indeed Michael Fullard, my friend of over 20 years, was given the responsibility of staying awake for the remainder of the journey. Cut to 5 minutes after we departed Palm Springs and Michael was snoring. Less than three minutes after that and everyone other than me was asleep. I drove the rest of the way in silence as James had turned the radio off in case the music disrupted their snooze! We reached Los Angeles fairly soon after, and I likened driving into LA at night like racing on the computer game Mario Kart, with the amount of neon flashing, overhead lighting, and cars on the road. It was quite an experience.

Finally, I recall numerous trips to Rome. We take our staff every year to a place outside of Rome for a retreat, to reflect, for CPD, and to help develop team bonds. Sometimes people fly out a day or two early or stay a few days afterwards because of meetings in Rome, attending conferences, or simply taking some annual leave. We stay in a former monastery, overlooking Lake Albano. It is idyllic, peaceful, and the perfect place to reflect and take stock of one's research, the general direction of the Jubilee Centre, or to focus on a specific task. Every trip we have been on has always been eventful, though. I have brought the wrong passport to the airport and not been able to fly, travelled to the wrong airport and had to hotfoot it across Rome at rush hour, and we have had various degrees of tears and cheers and everything in between when feedback sessions have been particularly gruelling. In 2010, pre-Jubilee Centre, we landed in Rome to be told that most airspace had closed behind us following the Eyjafjallajökull eruptions and subsequent ash cloud than engulfed much of Europe. Our return to England involved acquiring a 53-seater coach, collecting a wedding party from central Rome who had found out about our coach via Facebook, and a 24-hour drive to Calais, before boarding a ferry as a foot passenger. The story was published in the University of Birmingham staff magazine under the headline 'Professor Arthur rescues 52 people from Rome'. Other trips to Rome have included seeing both Pope Francis and Pope Benedict XVI, including Pope Benedict's final public appearances in 2013. For the serenity and peace of the surroundings, the trips are always memorable, and that is before we get to the rigours of the academic discussions. I will conclude this chapter with a note of thanks, to James for taking me on so many trips with him, to colleagues for their good will and good humour, and for their hard work to make every event, conference and foreign trip a success. We have never had a bad event in the Jubilee Centre, which reflects the amount of time, effort, and level of detail that goes into the planning for each one. We have worked hard to get staff at all levels to invest themselves and find purpose in the events, conferences, and wider impact work that we do, which I feel is reflected in what we have achieved.

IV

Reflections
and the Future

Centre Successes

This book offers a reflection on the ten years that the Jubilee Centre has existed for. The motivations for writing this book were to create an archive of events between 2012 and 2022, to document the journey that we have been on and to celebrate our successes in written form. We have celebrated many of those successes throughout the last decade, and I have tried to reference the most significant, as well as personally poignant, successes in this book already. James Arthur set the Jubilee Centre up to be successful in 2012. Jack Templeton and the JTF wanted, even expected, us to be successful when Dr Templeton envisaged the ten-year horizon project. The staff who have worked for the Jubilee Centre have contributed to those successes. Here, though, rather than continue with another section of self-congratulatory reflection, I want to offer some insight into both what the Jubilee Centre views as 'success', and also into the hard work and effort that goes into all of what we do, whether that is seen as successful or otherwise.

Defining success is something that we have challenged colleagues to do in the Jubilee Centre. That has been regardless of their roles as researchers, administrators, managers and Principal Investigators. To say that something has been 'a success' seems to be a common phrase across much of society, where it is used both to justify one's actions and endeavours in order to stay relevant or exert influence, and also as an expectation in that something was successful because it happened. An event occurred; therefore, its organisers can call it a success. Mostly, though, we have been more discerning in reflections and evaluations of what denotes 'success'. Perhaps this has come from working on fixed term grants with stated contractual outputs and outcomes with the funder, therefore ticking off each research report, event and teaching resource is the minimum requirement to deem a grant phase successful. Perhaps this discernment over how we determine success comes from instilling a mindset in colleagues that there is always more that we can be doing. By that, I mean that the area we work in, on character and virtues, is not simply transactional. We do not apply for a grant, win it and fulfil its obligations and then move on to something new. I have challenged Professional Services colleagues to define how they find success in their work. They often contribute to the major outputs of the Jubilee Centre but may not see their names on research reports, journal articles, or collections of conference papers. Character development itself is a lifelong process, to have been part of a research project that has had such a long and varied journey has required an outlook that sees both the short and long term at the same time; that sees the wood *and* the trees simultaneously. This is not easy to do, but has been a fundamental part of the Jubilee Centre philosophy with regards 'success'. To give an example of such dual thinking might help explain better what I mean.

I have reflected on the successes of our annual conference in the previous chapter. That has happened through much of the focus, attention to detail and administration, as well as the quality of the academic content of each event, but it also came through realising the original vision for the annual conference. When we organised the first one in 2012, we wanted to establish a conference that people would want to come back to; that would, over time, become self-sufficient. We have introduced a registration fee for delegates, which we have increased incrementally each year to contribute towards the costs of the conference, and to prepare delegates for the future. The short-term task in 2012 was to create a well-conceived conference; to attract the 'great and the good' to attend and to participate in, with a secondary vision that it would need to be something which they would want to come back to. The successes, then, are multiplied – which can be easy to forget when one is in the midst of administration of an event, or waiting for invited speakers to reply or respond to a call for papers. The trick has been to keep one's eye on the horizon and future conferences, so that we are setting things up as much as possible for them to happen with relative ease as much as we are consumed in the moment with attending to the details of the event at hand. We feel that Oriel is one of the strongest components to the Jubilee Centre armoury of activities and resources, and that has come through not just making one event a success, but also through grounding each one in the aims and vision of the Jubilee Centre.

A second example that comes to mind on how the Jubilee Centre has achieved its successes is that of our research project structure. Whilst each project is unique and bespoke in nature, there exists a set of underlying principles and a timeline that grounds each project in the aims and vision of the Jubilee Centre. These principles make our portfolio cohere and aim to make each project easier to engage with, particularly where colleagues may need to help, work across projects, or take over should someone leave before the end of the project or before the end of a grant phase. I have referenced the fixed term nature of four 33-month grant phases. Projects need to fit into the grant phase so we begin by tasking research teams to map out their projects on a timeline. Of course, when you ask for a project timeline and give the research team 33-months, so everyone always plans their report launches, publications and final wrap up for the 33rd month. Therefore, there is often a need to bring all of the timelines together, consider them as a whole and adapt them so that publications are spaced out across the final few months of a grant phase. This ensures that there is a sustained period of reporting and publication each phase, which helps boost the wider profile of the Jubilee Centre. It also eases the pressure on those tasked with bringing the publications together – often the management team and professional services colleagues – so that one is not reading, editing, proofing and disseminating 5 or more research reports at the same time.

We have turned staff over in the Jubilee Centre. Such turnover has been relatively normal given the fixed-term nature of most contracts, therefore staff have moved on both at the end of grant phases and mid-grant phase, so projects have needed to be constructed so that they are robust and resilient, so that when a person has departed, it has not been detrimental to the work. We have always adopted and employed a way of working in the Jubilee Centre that everyone should be aware of everyone else's work, as there will be times when colleagues are asked to support other pieces of work. For example, I was asked to take over was the *Flourishing From the Margins* project that considered the place and provision of character education in alternative provision and marginalised young people. The two researchers who began working on that project in the Service Britain phase both left the Jubilee Centre with a year to go in the grant phase. That project had already been pencilled in to report in month 32 of the grant phase, but there was still a lot to do in terms of trialling an intervention and undertaking a series of in-depth interviews, as well as then doing the data analysis, writing the report, finalising the teaching resources, producing a film and planning a launch. I was only really able to complete the work due to the things we had put in place during the grant phase that allowed for more sharing between projects and keeping all colleagues updated on progress and direction.

Researchers were asked to draft sections of the final report throughout the grant phase, rather than leaving everything until the writing up stage, which happened in Gratitude Britain. In this case, they provided an invaluable base for me to build from as I wrote up the report. We had established good relationships with a range of partner organisations through the project, many of whom had ensured their students had engaged with the teaching intervention and completed pre- and post-intervention surveys. It was not all plain sailing, though, as such is the fluctuating and changing nature of much of alternative provision and youth work, so there were instances where partners had not been able to ensure such completion of the intervention. So there was quite a lot of frantic paddling beneath the water to accompany the calm that came with publishing the report. Looking back at that year in 2017, for me, I think it was probably the busiest year that we have had. My personal situation influences a lot of the reasons I say that, as I began my PhD studies that year, decided to run my first (and only) marathon, and became a father for the first time. On top of that, I took on a second job bringing the *Flourishing From the Margins* project to a conclusion, and led the reporting to JTF at the end of the grant phase in November. That was all in addition to the day-to-day activities of the Jubilee Centre, developing a relationship with KFF through visits to Chicago and Milwaukee, publishing a new iteration of the *Framework*, hosting events at the House of Lords, recruiting new members of staff, meeting the Prime Minister of North Macedonia, and announcing that James had been made Officer of the Most Excellent Order of the British Empire. Even by Jubilee Centre standards, it was some year.

I hope that the two examples, here, reflect the point I have sought to get across. We have not always imposed the same approaches to communication, staff development, dissemination throughout the ten years for the sake of it. Where something has worked, and worked well, then we have looked to replicate it in future phases, or across other projects, if appropriate, but that is not always possible. Often the success of a particular output resides not in the output itself, but in the energy, enthusiasm and commitment that the staff and stakeholders have put into it. For example, the CPD programme 'Leading Character Education in Schools' – that 3,000 of participants have signed up to from over 65 countries – is a success not because of the online platform that we used, nor the Jubilee Centre materials that are referenced, but far more because of the energy and effort that those who created it put in during its development. Spending significant time in researching what makes a good CPD programme, engaging teachers and school leaders and listening to them in order to understand what they find engaging and useful from CPD programmes, and being concise yet thorough in reflecting the wealth of research, resources and other information that the Jubilee Centre holds has been fundamental to making that programme what it is. We don't replicate processes, training or programmes based solely on the basis that something we have done before was successful. For example, we don't currently hold monthly research committee meetings as the interactions between our current group of researchers do not necessitate it as a formal meeting. We discuss projects, methodologies, data collection and analysis more frequently and less formally than we did in the early phases. This reflects an adaptation to ways of working and getting the best from our staff.

The successes of the Jubilee Centre, then, are largely a reflection of the personal undertakings that went into creating the output, publication or event, as well as an organisational attitude to be world-leading. Often, we define success in outcome terms, rather than output – but sometimes it is important to do both. Success for one piece of work may simply be that we managed to create a resource that fits into the suite of Jubilee Centre teaching resources, not that it has to be accessed more times than the top downloaded resource, for example. Also, success for another piece of work may be defined by the impact that it goes on to have – months or even years after its creation. Such is the nature of academic research that there is a tendency to write up, publish, and move on, and either assume that something has had an impact, or neglect to employ meaningful dissemination strategies that could make it impactful. The benefit of having the security of multiple research grants, as well as retaining the commitment of the Jubilee Centre management team for extended periods of their careers to work across grant phases has helped enormously in terms of the Jubilee Centre's successes. I am talking mainly, here, about James Arthur, of course, as well as Kristján Kristjánsson, Tom Harrison, Danielle Edwards and myself. Andrew Peterson joined the Jubilee Centre as Deputy Director in 2018 and has made a big impression on things, as well as sharing the various management, teaching and research loads on others. To have a solid and longstanding leadership team, as well as everyone being exceptional and, yes, remarkable in their work, makes life a lot easier in terms of strategy, vision and seeing the bigger picture. It has been a pleasure to work with the leaders in the field, and I have learnt so much from all of them. I will follow this section with a short reflection on staff who have worked in the Jubilee Centre, acknowledge their contributions, and also reflect on some of the strategies to recruitment and selection that we have employed.

Staffing and Personal Achievements

Spending ten years in one centre – indeed twelve years working for the same boss – is a significant period of time. This feels more significant considering that it covers a particularly formative period of my life. I was 24 years old when I was first interviewed by James for the role of 'Research Secretary and PA', and started in post just after my 25th birthday. I turned 37 in January 2022, and in those 12 years I have moved house 3 times, gotten engaged, gotten married, become a father twice over, started and completed my MPhil studies, and have advanced with my PhD studies, as well as achieving various other personal milestones. The story of my first interview with James has become a bit of folklore in the Jubilee Centre, as it ended up setting the tone for many future interviews. I still remember it clearly – it was late December 2009, and I had been working in the Finance Office at the

University in the Student Fees team. I had left corporate banking during the credit crunch of 2008/09, having decided to take quite a significant backwards step financially in order to work at the University, as I wanted to pursue further academic study – but could not afford to study full-time. The role in Student Fees was fairly routine administration – chasing students to pay their tuition and accommodation fees, and liaising with different parts of the University to update a student's record, check if they were in attendance, and so on. It was a nice change from the cut throat world of corporate banking, but it was a six-month contract which I only ever saw as a stepping stone to something else. Student Fees wanted to extend my contract, but I put an application in to the School of Education. The job advert and further particulars gave little away regarding the academic that I would be working for, nor the project I'd be working on. It seemed a fairly generic role description, and something that I can see now had probably been put together very quickly with James wanting someone appointed 'ASAP'. As there was little by way of insight into the role, I couldn't prepare much for the interview. It was also a job at the same entry-level grade that I was already at, so I was confident that if I could get an interview, then I could convince a panel that I was appointable.

I walked into the interview room to be met by the panel of three people. In reality, they probably did introduce themselves, but in my memory, James didn't even let me sit down before telling me that I 'wasn't qualified to be here' and had only been shortlisted due to the redeployed status that I held as an internal candidate. Naturally, this put me on the backfoot and I then spent the next hour - of what was meant to be a twenty-minute interview - trying to convince James that I was appointable. I fought my corner. My memory tells me that I had reached a point of suggesting that we should call it quits if there were still doubts over my suitability when James said that I 'must realise that I was the preferred candidate' – a very 'James' way of presenting things; that it is for me to realise, not for him to state. I didn't realise it at the time, but it was a typically comment for James to make during interviews – frank and to the point, but also disarming as it removed any further feeling that I was in a battle to convince anyone of my abilities. I have sat with James on about 200 interview panels since then and can recall occasions when he has told candidates something similar. I can say that I have learnt more from James about the purpose and skills of interviewing than I have from anyone else. James went on to offer me the job – calling me back to his office afterwards to discuss the details of it. I recall him saying to me that he asked for loyalty from his staff, and it is something that I believe that I have always reflected in my work and in establishing a friendship with James. That is not loyalty out of any sense of duty or obligation, but a trustworthiness and reliability that underpins my approach to work. Such loyalty isn't blind, either. James has taught me better than anyone to see the bigger picture. Where one might get bogged down in the moment over a particular task, or a frustrating exchange with a peer, it is important to retain context and look at the horizon. Sometimes that is reminding oneself of what one is doing and for what reasons. Other times that is looking to the future and where one wants to get to. James often refer to having a 'mental map of how to get from A to B.' Whether that be in relation to study or career progression, James speaks it in reference to the benefits of good character development. I know that the phrase has helped me, and that hard work has been rewarded on my journey to 'B' in the Jubilee Centre.

James has said previously that he 'probably broke every HR rule in the book' when we recruited eight researchers, six professional members of staff and a Professor in 2012. There was no 'probably' about it – we did, and we coined the phrase that 'it is easier to ask for forgiveness than it is to ask for permission' with regards navigating the bureaucracy of higher education administration. Of course, for a centre that was dedicating itself to research in character and virtues, that is not the most virtuous sounding phrase, but it is not intended to inspire vicious behaviours. Ultimately, we were doing something that hadn't been done before in the SoE – and probably not in the College, nor at University-level, in terms of the scope, scale and speed with which things came about. Rules needed to be bent, broken, re-written and forgotten completely in all areas of work when required. It is not always that the ends need to justify the means, as I am sure that colleagues in Finance, HR and Procurement at the University will have thought was our approach over the years, but I think we have shone our own spotlight on some of the working practices and policies that existed in University administration and improved them because of our impatience. But I have given as much back as I could, too. I have spent hours in the office and at home writing job descriptions for posts at every level, scouring spreadsheets to forecast expenditure and report to funders, and often doing as much of the donkey-work as possible so that when we have leant on colleagues in different departments in order to get a post signed off at short notice, or a purchase order raised quickly, we have limited what we have needed to ask of them. I have learned the art of persuasion, with my own approach being to put forward a gentle and polite case for why someone should help us do something faster than they would like, or in a way that they wouldn't like, and being quietly relentless in ensuring that it gets done. I have applied such an approach to my own studies – with applications to study getting held up often for weeks or months within the different bureaucracies in the University – as my PhD application went through in just a few weeks, when the standard time is several months. I managed to push my MPhil application through in just 48 hours!

The word 'relentless' is one that comes up quite a lot in public life. I recall its use in the positive sense in relation to a sports team going on an extended run of good form, but it also reflects a more negative aspect of modern living, that navigating all of the different facets of life can often feel that things are relentless. It is, of course, vital to take regular breaks, reflect and evaluate, and indeed to celebrate achievements. Sometimes we haven't done that enough in the Jubilee Centre, but we are more than making up for it in 2022! Yet where one feels a sense of purpose in what they do and why they are doing it, so being relentless should feel more positive than negative. I am trying to capture another feature of working in the Jubilee Centre and how we have ensured that we have endured and achieved what we have for so long. I said earlier that we have been 'remarkable' in what we have achieved. I would add, here, that we have also been 'relentless'. We have tried to articulate that to new staff whenever they have joined us, in setting expectations and anticipations, within the limitations that fixed term contracts and grant phase dates place on recruitment. The realities of working in the Jubilee Centre have sometimes caught some colleagues off guard, or they have found a limit to how long they can keep pace with the relentlessness of Jubilee Centre life – all of which is absolutely fine. There is no judgement attached to this section at all. Indeed, I have reflected and wondered what my own development would have been like had I stepped away from the Jubilee Journey at any point. I haven't though, and I am proud of what I have been part of for so long. What has made us achieve what we have achieved for so long, though, has been the colleagues that have done huge amounts of heavy lifting over the years. James, of course, deserves all of the credit for everything that the Jubilee Centre has done, but in addition to that and from a personal perspective, I have learnt more from James than I have from anyone else. He has shown me what it is to have a vision and execute that vision with purpose. James has taught me many, many things not limited to the value of good hospitality, the need to set expectations early of others, but also to keep your expectations of yourself open. James had no idea that the Jubilee Centre would achieve what it has done, but he set out with a vision for success. We would be successful because we set our minds to achieve, not because someone else let us achieve.

To be surrounded by the leading scholars in the field, to be encouraged by them to write my own work, do research and collaborate is inspiring. To work with and be supervised by one of the best scholars in the field is motivating and rewarding, as much as it sometimes is unnerving. I am saying this here, as I still have work to do for my doctoral studies, but Kristján Kristjánsson is not only one of the most prolific writers I know, but his ability to present complex philosophical topics in accessible and engaging language is an artform. I was quite daunted when my doctoral studies led me into some of the heavier areas of emotion literature, but to have Kristján's *Virtuous Emotions* (2018) to hand has been a revelation and a blessing that I hope serves me well through to the completion of my doctoral studies. That is just one example, and we have engaged many of the luminaries in the field, but as much as James has led the way and the Jubilee Centre wouldn't exist without James, it also wouldn't be what it is today without Kristján and it is a pleasure to know him and work with him. Again, I can say the same for Tom Harrison. Tom was one of the first people that I met at a Learning for Life event in 2010, and I had no idea then that we would end up in the Jubilee Centre together so long later. I am a few years younger than Tom, and whilst we have different careers, I have learnt a lot from him. Tom is a shining example of how one can give to the Jubilee Centre and develop your career at the same time. Tom has gone from strength-to-strength from his original role as Director of Development – leading the practical and developmental work of the early years of the Jubilee Centre, through to directing the MA Character Education programme and excelling in his academic career. Tom is a great voice for the Jubilee Centre, and I recall a moment when we took our team to Villa Palazzola. As usual, the planned itinerary was soon ripped up as James suggested we take advantage of the good weather and move from the cold conference room to the warm terrace. Tom had to change his session on the spot from a formal presentation with slides to a more intimate focus group style presentation, which he did without missing a beat. Andrew Peterson joined the Jubilee Centre in 2018 and he has added an extra arm of academic insight that has helped us continue to grow and expand our work. We can talk football all day long, but I find Andrew, someone who is a senior figure in the field, one of the most approachable and amenable people I've ever met.

I can't go through and name everyone that I have worked with in the Jubilee Centre, but I have saved space for two more colleagues. Firstly, Danielle Edwards is the best administrator that I have worked with. Danielle showed great resilience initially as she applied for two posts before joining the Jubilee Centre in 2013. Danielle has made it a better and brighter place ever since her arrival. Her positive outlook is greatly missed at present, as she is on maternity leave for the year, but her quiet resolve, diligence and fortitude have benefitted the Jubilee Centre to unknown degrees. Danielle is a superb administrator, but could be an equally good academic. She often sees things that our researchers do not, corrects research reports that have passed through multiple academic hands before hers. She graduated her MA studies in 2020, and one comment from an external examiner suggested that the thesis had been written by someone who has a prosperous academic career ahead of them. This amused Danielle, as she has no intention of pursuing one, but she has personified the remarkable relentlessness that I have described above. She applies herself to all that she does for the benefit of the Jubilee Centre, and she has done so brilliantly. Secondly, I can't write a history of the Jubilee Centre and not mention my best friend Michael Fullard. Indeed, I have mentioned him already. Michael first joined the Jubilee Centre in 2015 as a Teaching Fellow, after I had suggested he apply to take a break from the classroom for a term. Michael is a primary school teacher, now turned academic researcher. Whilst I facilitated the introductions between Michael and James, I have always been reminded of the conflict of interest that working with a friend holds. I have not offered opinions on his suitability for posts; he has impressed enough on his own. In a similar vein to my first interview with James, Michael was asked a typically demanding question of 'what is your definition of ambition and why do you lack it?' Michael recovered from the shock of being asked enough to impress James to offer him an initial Teaching Fellowship and has shown sufficient ambition since then to stay in the Jubilee Centre. I did wonder what it would be like bringing someone from your personal life into your professional life, but it has probably brought us closer together as friends. It has been great to see Michael flourish in the Jubilee Centre, to grow as a researcher, and to lead on truly outstanding pieces of work such as the CPD programme. Our lives are very entwined, and we live less than half a mile from one another, but we are not (yet) sick of one another, and hope to see more of how we can benefit the Jubilee Centre and how it can benefit us.

I had only limited managerial experience when I became Centre Manager in 2012, as many of us at the time had limited or no experience of running a research centre. That experience has grown over the years, and we in the Jubilee Centre are well-versed in dealing with most matters of human resources, finance, administration and general management. As much as there have been some bumps in the road, the Jubilee Centre has been a success largely through the attention to detail we've paid when recruiting colleagues. As much as I have name-checked the management team of the Jubilee Centre, I also want to record my thanks and gratitude to those who I have managed. I try and help develop everyone that I have managed, and hope that those still in the Jubilee Centre and those who have moved on have felt supported by me. Management is hard. Well, it is hard as it is time consuming, emotionally engaging and sometimes draining and frustrating. However, they are the negatives. Management is also very rewarding, inspiring and invigorating. I tried to set a rule in the early years that I should not judge others by my standards. I know I set high standards of myself, and people have come into the Jubilee Centre at different times, for different reasons, with different perspectives, so I have taught myself that it is better as a manager to understand an individual's own expectations of themselves, and to encourage them to meet and exceed them. This has not always been easy, but we have had some remarkable people work in the Jubilee Centre, who have benefitted the research and professional work, and who I think would all reflect on what the Jubilee Centre has offered them. It is a special and somewhat unique place to work, which often comes with unstated privileges and benefits, but is world-leading in what it does, so requires a world-leading attitude to working in it.

Challenges

The past ten years have not all been plain sailing. There have been challenges and frustrations that have led us to the moments of celebration and success. Those challenges have been at all levels, from the administrative and bureaucratic challenges associated with establishing a large research centre in a university, through to academic challenges within and to our work. The whole act of establishing and maintaining a research centre seeking to impact policy, practice and scholarship on a global scale has, itself, been one big challenge. It is one that we have relished, at times become frustrated by, but generally been something that we have excelled at. Specific challenges have ranged from the obvious internal bureaucratic processes not happening quickly enough for our liking, to the unforeseen but predictable such as staff resignations and changes to reporting requirements. There have also been the challenges that we could neither predict nor effect, such has a constant rotation of secretaries of state and a global pandemic. Most of these are challenges that have not been unique to the Jubilee Centre, but the ways in which they have impacted us and the ways in which we have sought to overcome them are unique to us. During the course of ten years of recruitment, selection and retention of staff, we have created a resilience in our processes and within our staff to be able to absorb challenge and negotiate the hurdles of higher education administration. There have been times when the burdens of finding new ways to overcome the challenges of internal bureaucracies have fallen to one, two, or three people, or be limited to the Management Team; but that has both created a focus in our work to overcome the particular challenge at hand and protected others from needing to become involved. As we have evolved as a centre, for example creating the MA Character Education programme, so we were met with new challenges that we had little or no experience of overcoming. There have been times when we have needed to seek counsel from outside of the Jubilee Centre and outside of the University of Birmingham as to how best to go about something. The networks that we have created have helped support our endeavours, particularly when we have been able to draw on the experience of others to help overcome a particular challenge.

A lot of the challenges have come from doing a lot of things at the same time. We rarely settle as a management team and are always looking at what more we can do, such as establishing the world's first distance learning programme in character education, or opening the world's only secondary training school explicitly dedicated to character development. These have been huge undertakings in and of themselves, let alone as extras on top of delivering back-to-back multi-million-pound research grants. Looking back to some of those early days in 2012 when we thought we were busy recruiting to posts, or inducting new hires, those first six months or so of Gratitude Britain seem positively quiet by comparison to subsequent years. We have recruited new teams of researchers for each phase of work, often bringing colleagues in early at the end of a grant phase whilst managing that end of grant phase reporting period. Add into that in 2015 the opening of the University of Birmingham School, and in 2020 inducting new colleagues, reporting to funders, all whilst working remotely as enforced by the Covid-19 pandemic. Each year has been different, varied, and as challenging as it has been rewarding.

As well as completing our own work, and publishing the hundreds of reports, papers, chapters and books that have stemmed from the Jubilee Centre's work, we have been met with the challenge of academic disagreement. Often, this has helped stimulate discussion, within the Jubilee Centre, at conferences, but sometimes the criticism has felt somewhat one-eyed. We are not immune from criticism. Indeed, we welcome it, as it helps both with our own positioning of what character is, as well as being good for staff development to have their ideas and research critiqued by the leading scholars in the field. We regularly challenge our researchers on their knowledge of Jubilee Centre history, and where it is better to cite an internal publication when an idea or term has originated, and when it is better to cite an external publication or scholar who we have informed, or who has developed an idea or concept. We hold a lot of the global expertise on character within the Jubilee Centre. As a result, those leading the Jubilee Centre are often the best people for our researchers to learn from. We have also engaged all of the leading scholars around the world. We have hosted most of them in the Jubilee Centre, heard them speak and encouraged staff to learn from them, discuss and debate particular points, and even co-author publications together. In the spirit of academic debate, those collaborations and visits have been wholly positive and useful learning experiences for us all.

We do not claim to be the font of all knowledge on character, and where there has been academic challenge to our work, we have sought to use it to develop either our articulation and presentation of an idea, or to improve the rigour of the research that we undertake. However, we have found in more recent years a small number of written challenges to our work which have been intentionally selective in what authors have chosen for criticism. Interestingly, where we have reached out to authors to invite them to engage with us and discuss the challenges that they pose, they have, so far, been ignored or rejected. My point, here, isn't to either dismiss or even dwell on the academic criticism that we have received. It is to state that we aware that our work may provoke debate, and that it has limitations. We wish to engage with critical debates with the same intensity that we hold within the Jubilee Centre, but that has not always been possible. The field of character and virtues scholarship over the past ten years has developed by an untold amount. The rise in profile globally at academic, practice and policy levels has given character education great status. Funders are funding huge investments in new research and theoretical advancements and we hope that this remains for the foreseeable future. Equally, character has become a valued part of schooling, in and of itself and for its secondary impact on attainment, behaviour and other measurable variables. We hope, too, that this explicit focus remains, both at a practice and a policy level. The challenge, then, is to ensure that it does remain, endure, and develop. This is far more a challenge to ourselves than challenging perceptions that the Jubilee Centre definition of character is individualistic, rejects the civic virtues, or that our impact on policy has been achieved through any other means than encouraging policymakers to see character as a positive outcome of good education. As legitimate as each perspective might be, to single individual resources out without acknowledging the part they play in the whole picture limits one's argument. We have sought to engage those who offer criticisms and challenges of us, in order to learn and to improve, and will continue with this approach into the future.

To meet the challenges that are asked of us, there needs to be an acknowledgement that there is more to do – which we do. There needs to be areas to expand our research and teaching into – which there is. There needs to be a motivation and energy to continue – which there is. As such, then, the Jubilee Centre is well placed to meet its immediate challenges as we move through our tenth anniversary year, and towards the end of the original horizon project as envisaged by Jack Templeton.

The Future – Beyond 2023

No one can predict what the future holds, but we can say with certainty that Celebration Britain will run until 30th September 2023. We have work to do to accomplish the goals and outcomes of this grant phase, but we are well on the way to doing so at time of writing. This will complete 11-years and 4 months since the launch of the Jubilee Centre. After that, the Jubilee Centre will change. The MA Character Education will continue. The programme continues to develop and grow. The programme is a real tour-de-force, useful for both experienced academics looking to enhance their knowledge and understanding of character and for practitioners and early career academics looking to add academic theory to their exemplary practice. It is a jewel in the Jubilee Centre's crown and will continue to be beyond 2023.

The research programme of the Jubilee Centre post-2023 will move on from what has preceded it. It is a somewhat strange moment to pause and consider the future of the Jubilee Centre beyond Celebration Britain, to write it in this book. This book acknowledges the moment in time in 2022 and the decade that preceded it – as a decade worth celebrating. There is work still to do, though. Whilst there is work still to do, so we will put ourselves forward to do it. The development of character and virtues is a lifelong process, and so research into it will take just as long!

References

Aristotle (2002) *The Nicomachean Ethics* (Tr. Broadie, S. and Rowe, C.). Oxford: Oxford University Press.

Jubilee Centre for Character and Virtues (2013) *Gratitude Britain: One Year On*, Birmingham: Jubilee Centre for Character and Virtues, University of Birmingham.

Jubilee Centre for Character and Virtues (2017) *A Framework for Character Education in Schools*, Birmingham: Jubilee Centre for Character and Virtues, University of Birmingham.

Jubilee Centre for Character and Virtues (2022, forthcoming) *The Jubilee Centre's* Framework for Character Education in Schools*: Its Provenance and Rationale*, Birmingham: Jubilee Centre for Character and Virtues, University of Birmingham.

Lexmond, J. and Grist, M. (Eds) (2011) *The Character Inquiry*, London: Demos.

Thompson, A. and Metcalfe, J. (2020) 'Charting the character strengths of #iwill Ambassadors', *Impact: Journal of the Chartered College of Teaching*, November 2020. Available at: https://impact.chartered.college/article/charting-the-character-strengths-iwill-ambassadors/ (Accessed 1 December 2021).

Selected Publications
by the Jubilee Centre for Character and Virtues

CENTRE REPORTS

Arthur, J. and Earl, S. (2020) *Character in the Professions: How virtue informs practice*, Birmingham: Jubilee Centre for Character and Virtues, University of Birmingham.

Arthur, J., Earl, S., Thompson, A. and Ward, J. (2019) *Repurposing the Professions: The role of professional character*, Birmingham: Jubilee Centre for Character and Virtues, University of Birmingham.

Arthur, J., Edwards, D. and Thompson, A. (2020) *Transformation Through Character: December 2017 – January 2020*, Birmingham: Jubilee Centre for Character and Virtues, University of Birmingham.

Arthur, J., Fullard, M., Watts, P. and Moller, F. (2018) *Character Perspectives of Student Teachers*, Birmingham: Jubilee Centre for Character and Virtues, University of Birmingham.

Arthur, J., Harrison, T., Burn, E. and Moller, F. (2017) *Schools of Virtue: What works in character education*, Birmingham: Jubilee Centre for Character and Virtues, University of Birmingham.

Arthur, J., Harrison, T., Carr, D., Kristjánsson, K., Davidson, I., Hayes, D., Higgins, J. and Davidson, J. (2014) *Knightly Virtues: Enhancing virtue literacy through stories*, Birmingham: Jubilee Centre for Character and Virtues, University of Birmingham.

Arthur, J., Harrison, T., Kristjánsson, K., Davison, I., Hayes, D., Higgins, J. and Ryan, K. (2014) *My Character: Enhancing future-mindedness in young people,* Birmingham: Jubilee Centre for Character and Virtues, University of Birmingham.

Arthur, J., Harrison, T. and Taylor, E. (2015) *Building Character Through Youth Social Action,* Birmingham: Jubilee Centre for Character and Virtues, University of Birmingham.

Arthur, J., Harrison, T., Taylor-Collins, E. and Moller, F. (2017) *A Habit of Service: The factors that sustain service in young people,* Birmingham: Jubilee Centre for Character and Virtues, University of Birmingham.

Arthur, J., Kristjánsson, K., Cooke, S., Brown, E. and Carr, D. (2015) *The Good Teacher: Understanding virtues in practice,* Birmingham: Jubilee Centre for Character and Virtues, University of Birmingham.

Arthur, J., Kristjánsson, K., Gulliford, L., Morgan, B. and Roberts, R. C. (2015) *An Attitude for Gratitude: How gratitude is understood, experienced and valued by the British public,* University of Birmingham: Jubilee Centre for Character and Virtues.

Arthur, J., Kristjánssson, K., Thomas, H., Holdsworth, M., Badini Confalonieri, L. (2014) *Virtuous Character for the Practice of Law,* Birmingham: Jubilee Centre for Character and Virtues, University of Birmingham.

Arthur, J., Kristjánsson, K., Thomas, H., Kotzee, B., Ignatowicz, A., Qiu, T. and Pringle, M. (2015) *Virtuous*

Medical Practice, Birmingham: Jubilee Centre for Character and Virtues, University of Birmingham.

Arthur, J., Kristjánsson, K., Walker, D., Sanderse, W., Jones, C., Thoma, S., Curren, R., Roberts, M. and Lickona, T. (2015) *Character Education in UK Schools,* Birmingham: Jubilee Centre for Character and Virtues, University of Birmingham.

Arthur, J., Moulin-Stożek, D., Metcalfe, J. and Moller, F. (2019) *Religious Education Teachers and Character: Personal beliefs and professional approaches,* Birmingham: Jubilee Centre for Character and Virtues, University of Birmingham.

Arthur, J., Thompson, A., Kristjánsson, K., Moller, F., Ward, J. and Rogerson, L. (2017) *Flourishing From the Margins: Living a good life and developing purpose in marginalised young people,* Birmingham: Jubilee Centre for Character and Virtues, University of Birmingham.

Arthur, J., Thompson, A. and Wartnaby, D. (2015) *From Gratitude to Service: Engagement, Influence and Impact June 2012 – February 2015,* Birmingham: Jubilee Centre for Character and Virtues, University of Birmingham.

Arthur, J., Wartnaby, D., Ward, J. and Thompson, A. (2018) *Shaping the Future: Impacting policy and practice,* Birmingham: Jubilee Centre for Character and Virtues, University of Birmingham.

Arthur, J., Walker, D. I. and Thoma, S. (2018) *Soldiers of Character,* Birmingham: Jubilee Centre for Character and Virtues, University of Birmingham.

Barrett, A., Maxfield, S. and Wright, P. (2015) *Good Neighbours in a Good Neighbourhood? An exploration of gratitude in a local community*, Birmingham: Jubilee Centre for Character and Virtues, University of Birmingham.

Demos and Jubilee Centre for Character and Virtues (2015) *Character Nation: A Demos report with the Jubilee Centre*, London: DEMOS.

Demos and Jubilee Centre for Character and Virtues (2017) *The Moral Web: Youth, character, ethics and behaviour*, London: DEMOS.

Fullard, M. and Watts, P. (2020) *Leading Character Education in Schools: An online CPD programme*, Birmingham: Jubilee Centre for Character and Virtues, University of Birmingham.

Gulliford, L. and Morgan, B. (2016) *Taking Thanks for Granted: Unravelling the concept of gratitude in a developmental cross-cultural analysis*, Birmingham: Society for Educational Studies.

Harrison, T., Dineen, K. and Moller, F. (2018) *Parent-Teacher Partnerships: Barriers and enablers to collaborative character education*, Birmingham: Jubilee Centre for Character and Virtues, University of Birmingham.

Harrison, T., Hayes, D. and Higgins, J. (2015) *An Exploration of Gratitude in the Thank You Film Awards*, Birmingham: Jubilee Centre for Character and Virtues, University of Birmingham.

Harrison, T., Hunter, R., Miller, B., with Metcalfe, J. (2020) *An Evaluation of a Workshop for Parents and Teachers on Character Education,* Birmingham: Jubilee Centre for Character and Virtues, University of Birmingham.

Harrison, T. and Khatoon, B. (2017) *Virtue, Practical Wisdom and Professional Education: A pilot intervention designed to enhance virtue knowledge, understanding and reasoning in student lawyers, doctors and teachers,* Birmingham: Jubilee Centre for Character and Virtues, University of Birmingham.

Harrison, T. and Polizzi, G. (2021) *A Cyber-Wisdom Approach to Digital Citizenship Education,* Birmingham: Jubilee Centre for Character and Virtues, University of Birmingham.

Jubilee Centre for Character and Virtues (2013) *Gratitude Britain: One Year On,* Birmingham: Jubilee Centre for Character and Virtues, University of Birmingham.

Kristjánsson, K., Arthur, J., Moller, F. and Huo, Y. (2017) *Character Virtues in Business and Finance,* Birmingham: Jubilee Centre for Character and Virtues, University of Birmingham.

Kristjánsson, K., Darnell, C., Fowers, B., Moller, F., and Pollard, D., with Thoma, S. (2020) Phronesis*: Developing a conceptualisation and an instrument,* Birmingham: Jubilee Centre for Character and Virtues, University of Birmingham.

Kristjánsson, K., Gulliford, L., Arthur, J. and Moller, F. (2017) *Gratitude and Related Character Virtues*, Birmingham: Jubilee Centre for Character and Virtues, University of Birmingham.

Kristjánsson, K., Pollard, D. and Darnell, C. (2021) Phronesis: *Using an Aristotelian model as a research tool*, Birmingham: Jubilee Centre for Character and Virtues, University of Birmingham.

Kristjánsson, K., Thompson, A. and Maile, A. with Ritzenthaler, S. and Moller, F. (2021) *Character Virtues in Policing*, Birmingham: Jubilee Centre for Character and Virtues, University of Birmingham.

Kristjánsson, K., Varghese, J., Arthur, J. and Moller, F. (2017) *Virtuous Practice in Nursing*, Birmingham: Jubilee Centre for Character and Virtues, University of Birmingham.

Peterson, A. and Civil, D. with Ritzenthaler, S. (2021) *Educating for Civic Virtues and Service: School Leader Perspectives*, Birmingham: Jubilee Centre for Character and Virtues, University of Birmingham.

Rogerson, L. (2015) G*ive Thanks - Give Back: Gratitude and service in school and the community*, Birmingham: Jubilee Centre for Character and Virtues, University of Birmingham.

Sweeney, P., Prince, L., Nailer, E., Morgan, B., Gulliford, L., Orangers, K. and Tinari, C. (2016) *Torchbearers of Liberty: An evaluation of education interventions aimed to teach liberty and its pillar virtues,*

Birmingham: Jubilee Centre for Character and Virtues, University of Birmingham.

Thompson, A. and Edwards, D. (2019) *The Prince William Award: A qualitative evaluation*, Birmingham: Jubilee Centre for Character and Virtues, University of Birmingham.

CENTRE FRAMEWORKS AND STATEMENTS

Jubilee Centre for Character and Virtues (2014) *Statement on Youth Social Action and Character Development*, Birmingham: Jubilee Centre for Character and Virtues, University of Birmingham.

Jubilee Centre for Character and Virtues (2015) *Statement on Teacher Education and Character Education*, Birmingham: Jubilee Centre for Character and Virtues, University of Birmingham.

Jubilee Centre for Character and Virtues (2016) *Statement on Character, Virtue and Practical Wisdom in Professional Practice*, Birmingham: Jubilee Centre for Character and Virtues, University of Birmingham.

Jubilee Centre for Character and Virtues (revised, 2017) *A Framework for Character Education in Schools*, Birmingham: Jubilee Centre for Character and Virtues, University of Birmingham.

Jubilee Centre for Character and Virtues (2019) *Statement on Civic Virtues in the Public Domain*, Birmingham: Jubilee Centre for Character and Virtues, University of Birmingham.

Jubilee Centre for Character and Virtues (2020) *Statement on Character and Sport*, Birmingham: Jubilee Centre for Character and Virtues, University of Birmingham.

Jubilee Centre for Character and Virtues and The Oxford Character Project (2020) *Character Education in Universities: A Framework for Flourishing*, Birmingham: Jubilee Centre for Character and Virtues, University of Birmingham.

Jubilee Centre for Character and Virtues (2021) *Statement on Character and the Pandemic*, Birmingham: Jubilee Centre for Character and Virtues, University of Birmingham.